BERNARD EDWARD ISON

Amazing Saints

ST PAULS

ST PAULS Publishing
187 Battersea Bridge Road
London SW11 3AS, UK

Copyright © ST PAULS 2000

ISBN 085439 581 4

Set by TuKan DTP, Fareham, UK
Printed by Interprint Ltd, Marsa, Malta

ST PAULS is an activity of the priests and brothers
of the Society of St Paul who proclaim the Gospel
through the media of social communication

AMAZING SAINTS

Contents

Introduction

For more years than I care to remember, the saints have been a source of inspiration and a cause for admiration. We all need heroes; the encouragement of knowing that if *they* can do it, then *we* can do it. We applaud the holiness and joy of the saints as they fought the battle of life with a devotion *we* can only envy. What rare courage they displayed, solely inspired by a loving commitment to the Saint of Saints who died for us on the cross!

Each of the saints followed Christ to a personal Calvary... and in a variety of ways. Some were hermits or monks, some were mystics and great penitents, kings and queens, workers of miracles. Many were tortured and suffered martyrdom. Among them there are those who appear to be touched by a celestial stardust, capture the imagination and are strikingly unique and utterly amazing – these are my AMAZING SAINTS.

St Simon Stylites

(AD 459)

January 5

Simon was a poor shepherd boy who lived on the borders of Syria where he looked after his father's sheep. One day when he was thirteen years of age, he heard the Beatitudes read out at church, and he asked an old man what they meant. How was the happiness they promised to be obtained? The old man told him that prayer and fasting and patient suffering were the road to *true* happiness and a solitary life was the best way to practise these good works.

Simon prayed that God would help him find the path which led to happiness and perfection, and eventually he found himself at the gates of a monastery in the neighbourhood which was under the direction of a holy abbot named Timothy. For several days Simon waited to be admitted without eating or drinking and after a time he was admitted, as a novice.

Though only a boy he practised the austerities of the house before he was transferred to the monastery of Heliodorus. Here Simon increased his mortifications. Such was his love for the sufferings of Jesus Christ, he wore a rough piece of rope from a well bucket bound tightly round his waist. After a time the rope bit deep into his flesh but when this was discovered, due to the stench from the wound, a physician was required to cut the rope out from the flesh. Such was his anguish and pain that for a long time he lay as if dead.

When he had recovered the abbot, fearful of similar occurrences within the monastery, dismissed him.

Simon went to a hermitage at the foot of Mount Telnescin. In his first Lent he decided to pass the whole forty days in total abstinence after the example of Christ, without eating or drinking.

His spiritual director, Bassus, a holy priest and abbot of over two hundred monks, knew of his intentions, so he left him ten loaves of bread, and water so that he might eat and drink if he found it necessary. At the end of the forty days, Bassus came to visit him; he found the loaves and water untouched and Simon stretched out on the ground with no sign of life. Taking a sponge, Bassus moistened his lips with water then gave him Holy Communion. Simon recovered, sat up and chewed, then swallowed herbs and lettuce leaves.

In this way, Simon would keep every Lent for the rest of his life.

After three years in the hermitage, Simon climbed to the top of Mount Telnescin and there he made himself a shelter with stones, but without a roof. There he lived in solitude with only God as his companion, yet his solitude was interrupted as pilgrims from near and far came to visit him and receive his blessing. Many of the sick recovered their health, but the throngs of people were the cause of many distractions, so to regain his solitude, in the year 423, Simon erected a pillar six cubits high (about three metres) and on it he lived for the next four years. Here he was brutally exposed to the sweltering heat of the day, the wind and rain, and the biting cold of the night. On a second pillar, twelve cubits high, he lived for three years. On a third, twenty-two cubits high, he lived for ten years and on a fourth, built for him by the people and forty cubits high, he spent the last twenty years of his life.

So he lived for a total of thirty-seven years on pillars called Stylites, from the Greek word *Stylos*, which signifies a pillar.

Simon's pillar was only about a metre across at the top, which made it impossible for him to lie down, and neither would he have a seat. His garments were the skins of wild animals and he wore an iron collar around his neck. He prayed continually, and twice a day he preached to the people gathered below him.

Many were converted by his exhortations and miracles: barbarians, Persians, Armenians, princes and queens of the Arabians came to receive his blessing. Vararanes the King of Persia, though a cruel tyrant, respected him. The Emperors Theodosius and Leo often consulted him and begged his prayers, the Emperor Marcian visited him and Domnus, patriarch of Antioch often took Holy Communion to him.

By an invincible patience, Simon bore all afflictions and for a long time concealed a horrible ulcer in his foot swarming with maggots. Considering himself to be an outcast of the world and a sinner, he spoke to all with great kindness and love.

In 459 Simon, the incomparable penitent and supreme example of humility died at the age of sixty-nine. His body was taken down from his pillar and then to Antioch for burial and, it is related, many miracles were wrought. A fitting climax to an extraordinary life of devotion, motivated by an overwhelming love for our Lord and Saviour, Jesus Christ.

St Augustine of Hippo

(AD 430)
August 28

To discover the great St Augustine is to reveal a man unique in his contradictions. His father was an idolater, his mother was a Christian. He was a heretic who became one of the great theologians of the Church. A sinner who really enjoyed his sins (he was in no hurry to repent) yet was later to become a saint. An intellectual who thought he was clever enough to solve the mystery of life – and couldn't. A wayward son saved by the prayers and the amazing love of Monica his devoted mother.

Monica (also to become a saint) was the wife of Patricius who was an easygoing minor government official and a pagan. She came from a respectable middleclass family. The marriage was a success, and Monica did not have to endure the intermittent beatings inflicted by most husbands of the day on their wives. There were three children: Augustine, Navigius and a daughter whose name has been lost in history.

Augustine was born in 354 at Tagaste, near the city of Hippo in North Africa. When he reached the age of twelve he attended a School of Grammar (Greek and Latin) and at seventeen he was sent to Carthage. As it was not the custom in those days to baptise infants, Augustine was not baptised, despite his mother's prayers and influence. So, a Christian he wasn't but a prodigy he certainly was, with a huge capacity for study and Latin as his forte.

He also liked a good time and under the influence of his lusty companions he took a mistress, as was the fashion among young people. Before he was twenty years of age he was the father of a boy, Adiodatus.

Shortly after this he became a Manichaean, a sect which had infiltrated the Catholic Church and who mocked its authority. They believed, among other things. that 'they could lead men to God and free them from error by reason alone'.

Then in 371 Augustine's father, Patricius, died. Yet shortly before his death the prayers of his wife had been answered: Augustine had been baptised a Catholic.

Augustine continued his studies at Carthage, then after nine years he became disillusioned with the Manichean sect and, utterly disgusted with the behaviour of the pupils at the school where he taught, he decided to move to Rome. Despite Monica's tearful protestations that he should stay, he sneaked away when the opportunity arose. In Rome he hoped to solve his spiritual problems; instead he found illness, only to be saved from death by the prayers of his devoted mother. Augustine was acclaimed by the scholars and the learned yet he decided the great city of Rome was not for him. Fortunately, his reputation as a teacher had spread and in 384 he accepted an invitation to lecture in Milan. Here he was joined by his mother who begged him to marry and settle down. (She had, in fact, a very young girl lined up for him.) Augustine responded by rejecting his mistress (probably at the instigation of Monica) and sending her back to Africa. But he kept his son with him, much to the delight of Monica and then took another mistress, much to her displeasure.

In Milan Augustine was a tremendous success, confirming his high esteem among the intellectuals. Ambrose, the Bishop of Milan (later to become St Ambrose) heard him with respect. Augustine was anxious to meet the renowned bishop, not because he was a teacher of the truth but only because he was a man of great learning and reputation. He often attended the bishop's sermons and, deep down in his heart, these words sowed the seed of faith.

For a time Augustine dabbled in the works of Plato only to find they bred pride in his heart, not humility. Then, perhaps affected by the words of the holy bishop he began to study the New Testament – especially the writings of St Paul. Augustine was close to becoming a Catholic, yet the weight of his sins deterred him and he could not break free from the vice of impurity, accepting that he actually *enjoyed* his sin. His soul cried out for conversion but his body said no! Perhaps his dilemma could be best expressed by a few lines of verse we could call Augustine's Theme:

Thou knowest that I love thee Lord,
Yet find it hard to keep thy word.
Temptation I don't want to fight,
Will I ever see the light?
But there's always time – I'll change you know,
I'll wear a halo white as snow.
And when I'm old I'll put things right,
As sure as sunrise follows night.
I'll try my best to pay the debt,
Lord make me good – but please, not yet.

Augustine had the care of a young pupil named Alypius and one day they were together in a garden. Augustine, despondent and tearful, had moved away to find solitude. Tormented by his passion for sin and his search for the true faith he suddenly heard a child singing from a house nearby. Over and over the small, sweet voice repeated the refrain:

'*Take it and read...*
Take it and read...'

Augustine stood up, wiped the tears from his eyes and telling himself this was a divine command, he went back to where Alypius was waiting, to his book of sacred scripture and read at the place where the book fell open: '...not in revelling and drunkeness; not in debauchery and licentiousness, not in quarrelling and jealousy but put on the Lord Jesus Christ and make no provision for the flesh, to gratify its desires.'

As he read, a light of confidence shone into his whole being and all the darkness of doubt was dispelled. Augustine travelled to Cassiciacum with Monica and a group of friends and from there he wrote to Bishop Ambrose asking to be received into the Church. He was baptised at Easter, 387 together with his son Adiodatus and his pupil Alypius. In the pursuit of spirituality and solitude they set out to return to Africa, but at Ostia while waiting for a ship, Monica became ill and died at the age of fifty-six.

From her deathbed she had instructed Augustine and Navigius: 'Lay this body anywhere, be not concerned about that. The only thing I ask is that you remember me before the altar of God.'

So Monica slept in ultimate contentment; her prayers had won her son back to God. Augustine was thirty-two years old, and her death engulfed him in tears as he recalled the tender and affectionate care of her children, and her persistent and devout prayers for his own conversion.

Augustine and his friends made their way to Tagaste and settled there on the family estate. Here they lived a communal life of study and prayer but a year later tragedy struck again: Adiodatus died at the age of seventeen.

Augustine was devastated. For the next three years he stayed at Tagaste, deep in his devotions, with occasional visits to Hippo. Valerius, the bishop of that city had proclaimed to the people the need to ordain a priest for service in the Church. So when Augustine one day appeared in the church he was manhandled by the crowd and taken before Valerius to be ordained. Augustine was overwhelmed in humility – he burst into tears protesting his unworthiness but eventually he was ordained priest.

From that time on he was a changed man. After a period of solitude and recollection he took up his priestly duties and he began to preach... and preach, hundreds of sermons, partly to help out Bishop Valerius who, as a stranger, had difficulty with the local language. He preached to greater and greater acclaim with an eloquence and influence acknowledged superior to that of the renowned Cicero.

After one particular sermon, Firmus, a rich and zealous patron of the Manichees, cast himself at the feet of Augustine to be converted on the spot. He later became a priest.

Bishop Valerius, advancing in years and infirmities, arranged with Aurelius, the Archbishop of Carthage that Augustine should succeed him. So when the good bishop died in the following year, Augustine did indeed succeed him to become Bishop of Hippo at the age of forty-one. From then on his influence spread beyond the bounds of Africa yet his was a life of penance and mortification, of exemplary charity, so much so that at times sacred vessels were melted down and sold and the money used to reclaim prisoners.

This was also a time of literary endeavours for Augustine as he wrote book after book.

Confessions, his autobiography and a memorial of his deep repentance was written 397-398. The twenty-two books of *The City of God* were completed intermittently by 426. They explain the Creator's working in history, and are also remarkable for Augustine's conception of the creation of the world.

It was also a time of challenge to the authority of the Church, a time for Augustine to refute the false doctrines of the Donatists, the Manichees, the Arians, the Pelagians, Priscillianists and the Origenians. To the Jews he proved how the Mosaic law was to have an end and be changed into the New Law. For the Manichees he answered the question which had puzzled theologians for years: 'Whence came evil?' Augustine propounded that evil had no beginning of its own but came from the free will of man.

By the year 430 the Roman Empire in Africa was beginning to crumble and the siege of Hippo had begun. The fate of the city was sealed and the inhabitants faced the terrible situation with fear and dread, yet

Augustine remained a symbol of hope and courage. He was also a dying man. His final message from his deathbed expressed a divine sense of purpose: 'These are difficult and dreadful times but these times are a part of us. The times are what we have made of them. Yes, we are all guilty, but we have been promised mercy. Have you not been baptised in hope? Do you not understand that God's will can be accomplished through the most frightful afflictions?'

Augustine begged God's forgiveness for his sins and reproached himself for not having done enough for him; over and over he repeated the verses of the penitential psalms. Outside the city walls the Vandals threatened ever closer, the siege was about to erupt into its inevitable climax... and Augustine calmly resigned his spirit into the hands of God. It was August 28, the year was 430 and he was seventy-six years old.

He made no will and left no possessions, yet he did leave hope for all sinners. As sinners we can easily identify with Augustine, the sinner who became a saint.

He is the patron saint of theologians.

The Carthusian Martyrs of England
(1535)

The year of Our Lord 1535 was probably one of the most significant in the history of England. On 1 February of that year, the Act of Supremacy came into force, declaring it high treason to deny that the monarch was the supreme head of the Church in England. This was a dramatic turn of events. That King Henry VIII had been a good Catholic monarch in the tradition of Alfred the Saxon, St Edward the Martyr and Edward the Confessor could not be denied. His staunch defence of an ailing Catholic Church in the early years of his reign had earned him the title of 'Defender of the Faith' from the Pope – the *'Fid Def'* which is still to be found on coins of the realm.

Now the Catholic Church was outlawed and the Protestant religion, inspired by the flawed doctrines of the renegade monk Martin Luther, was to take its place, a religion sympathetic to the king's intention of divorcing his wife. This would now be the official religion of the realm; dissent in any form would not be tolerated and on that fateful day in February 1535, the battle lines were drawn in a contest which would pit the might of the king against the faith of the Church.

So England became a land divided into official Protestants and persecuted Catholics. King Henry, and later his successors, were confident that if they could exterminate the old Catholic clergy, then the Catholic

Church in England would die. The Catholic Church responded by instituting seminaries on the Continent to train young men who would return to England as missionary priests to keep the old religion alive.

The authorities soon realised what was happening and the chase was on. Richard Topcliffe, a savage hater of Catholics was to lead the priest hunters, spies and informers, with George Eliot, a renegade Catholic, being the most insidious and successful agent of all.

In an atmosphere dripping with menace the priests used false names, disguises, passwords and met in secret to say Mass and administer the Sacraments. They were constantly on the move up and down the country, on horseback, on foot, always ready to run or to hide and at times to totally disappear for a while. This was not too difficult as the population of England at that time was in the region of only two and a half million people. On occasion they were concealed in safe houses and many of the large country houses of the Catholic gentry were riddled with ingenious hiding holes, the inspiration and work of Nicholas Owen, a Jesuit lay brother.

The priests used any means to survive, to stay at liberty for the sake of the souls of the faithful. For those who were taken and refused to submit, the consequences were truly horrendous. Yet in spite of dungeon, fire and sword, the rack and the rope, priests and laity displayed a kind of outrageous courage which could only have been inspired by the Grace of God.

The first blow against the holy Catholic men fell in April 1535. Thomas Cromwell, King Henry's chief hatchetman ordered the arrest of three leading members of the Carthusian order: the Prior of London

Charterhouse, John Houghton, and Priors Robert Lawrence and Augustine Webster. They were confined in the Tower of London and on April 28 they were tried and condemned at Westminster Hall for refusing to take the Oath of Supremacy.

It was Cromwell's intention to make an example of these Church leaders and so terrify other religious into submission. Every effort was made to degrade them, even dragging them on hurdles to Tyburn in their religious habits where the executions were to be carried out. They were watched from a window in the Tower by Sir Thomas More and their example fortified his unwavering determination to die for the supremacy of the Pope, the successor of St Peter and Our Lord Jesus Christ.

When they arrived at the gallows, Prior John Houghton freely pardoned the executioner. As he stood on the cart with the rope around his neck he was offered, along with the others, a free pardon if he would take the Oath of Supremacy. He preferred death. A specially thick rope was used to make sure he was still alive when they cut him down. Robert Lawrence and Augustine Webster, with Richard Reynolds and John Haile who were also to be executed had to watch as they tore off his habit and the butchery began.

The five lifeless bodies were beheaded, hearts torn out and their remains chopped into quarters to be displayed as a warning in various districts of London. Yet their courage had been sustained right to the bitter end by the Mass of the Holy Spirit they had concelebrated when they knew their time had come, and by the well-known incident of a sudden 'gentle wind' passing through the chapel, which all present felt and believed was a visible manifestation of the Holy Spirit, come to strengthen their resolution.

The fate of these holy men on 8 May 1535, was a tragic overture to the terrifying events which were now about to commence.

St Mary of Egypt

(5th century)
April 9

In Palestine, in the reign of King Theodosius, there lived a holy monk and priest named Zosimus, famed for the reputation of his sanctity and his fervour for the religious life. He had served God from his youth, living in the same monastery for thirty-five years, and he was tempted to believe that he had reached such a state of perfection that no one could teach him anything about the monastic life.

God, in a revelation, directed him to a monastery near the River Jordan and it was there that he realised he was mistaken about his own heights of perfection. The members of this community had no contact with the outside world, chiefly existing on bread and water. They spent all their days in manual labour and prayer and most of the night in singing psalms and praising God.

It was their annual custom on the first Sunday of Lent to cross the River Jordan and disperse themselves over the vast deserts of Arabia, pass the time in perfect solitude till Palm Sunday and meet again at the monastery for Easter Sunday. During this time they existed on whatever little food they had taken with them or lived on the herbs which grew wild.

About the year 430, Zosimus crossed the Jordan with the others, to penetrate as far as he could into the vast wilderness. Here he was hoping to meet some hermit of still greater perfection and he prayed with great fervour as he travelled.

Having journeyed for twenty days he stopped one day at noon to recite the customary psalms and saw in the distance what he thought was a body, naked and extremely sunburnt; yet the body fled away from him.

Zosimus, thinking it was some holy hermit ran after him, shouting for the person to stop and bless him, but he was dumbfounded when the person cried: 'Zosimus, I am a woman. Throw me your cloak that I may cover myself.'

Zosimus was amazed that she knew his name and realised that she could only have known this by revelation. He threw his cloak to her and when she had wrapped it around her they spoke and prayed together. Then Zosimus asked her who she was.

'I should die from shame,' the woman began. 'My country is Egypt. When I was young, I ran away to Alexandria and fell into grievous sin. For seventeen years I was a prostitute; eventually I travelled to the Holy Land, still plying my trade, till we arrived in Jerusalem. When the pilgrims were going into the church for the great festival I mixed in with them, but when they crowded in to venerate the Holy Cross I found I could not follow – I was held back by some invisible force. This happened three times, then I realised my wickedness was the cause and I melted into tears.

'Looking up, I saw a picture of the mother of God. I begged her to pray for me that my repentance would be acceptable to God. I asked that I might be allowed to enter the church to venerate the sacred wood of the Cross.

'After my ardent prayer, a feeling of great consolation came over me and I was able to enter the church and venerate the glorious Cross.

'When I came out from the church, I fell down on my knees before the image of the mother of God and begged her to be my guide. After my prayer I seemed to hear a voice: "If you go beyond the Jordan, you will find rest and comfort".

'I begged of the holy queen that she would never abandon me.

'I bought three loaves of bread and asked the baker which gate of the city led to the Jordan. I immediately took the road which led to the Jordan and walked all the rest of the day. That night I slept on the ground and in the morning I crossed the Jordan, and from that time I have carefully shunned any human being.'

Zosimus asked how long she had been in the desert.

'As far as I can judge it is forty-seven years,' she replied.

'And how have you existed through all this time?'

'On the loaves I brought with me and on what I could scavenge in this wild, uncultivated land. My clothes wore out and I have suffered much from the heat and the cold, sometimes so much that I was unable to stand. I was tempted much and when I had not a drop of water to quench my thirst I longed for the luxuries of Egypt. My devotion to the Blessed Virgin delivered me.

'Now I have given you an account of myself, tell no one during my life. You are the only living person I have spoken to since I came into this wilderness. Remember me in your prayers.'

She concluded by asking Zosimus to bring Holy Communion to her on the banks of the Jordan the following Maundy Thursday. Then she left him.

Zosimus fell on his knees to kiss the ground where she had stood, then returned to his monastery.

The following Maundy Thursday, Zosimus took the sacred Body and Blood of Our Lord in a small chalice and set out for the Jordan. He also took a little basket of figs, dates and lentils

At night she appeared on the other side and, making the sign of the cross over the river, she walked across the surface of the water as if it were dry land.

Zosimus recited the Creed and the Lord's Prayer, then he gave her Holy Communion. She lifted up her arms to heaven and cried: 'Now thou dost dismiss thy servant O lord, according to thy word in peace; because my eyes have seen my Saviour.'

She thanked Zosimus and begged him to return the following Lent to the place where they had first met. Then she went back over the river as she came.

Zosimus returned home, but came back the following Lent as she had requested, determined to discover her name. On his arrival at the place where he had first seen her, he found her corpse stretched on the ground – with an inscription declaring her name to be Mary, and the time of her death.

Zosimus, miraculously assisted by a lion dug her grave and buried her. He then returned to his monastery where he told of all that he had heard and seen of Mary, the holy penitent. And there he continued to serve God till his happy death in his hundredth year.

St Alban

(AD 303)
June 22

The Christian faith had arrived in Britain in the time of the Apostles, and the conversion of King Lucius in 180 substantially helped to increase its numbers. Mercifully, the brutal persecutions in the Roman Empire had passed Britain by, until the murderous reign of the Emperor Diocletion. The first of the Christian heroes was Alban. He was of noble Roman origin and a native of Verulam, one of the principal cities in Britain at the time. (After many sieges by the Saxons it later fell into decay to be replaced by the present St Albans to which our saint gave his name.)

In his youth, Alban often travelled to Rome as part of his education before he finally settled in Verulam, to become one of its leading citizens. A pagan, yet a man of kindly nature, he gave shelter in his home to a Christian priest when the persecution of Diocletion was at its height. So impressed was he by the holy deportment of the priest Amphibalus, by his faith and assiduous prayer, that Alban was baptised to become a Christian.

He had sheltered the priest for many days when soldiers, acting on information received, arrived at Alban's house to arrest the priest. Alban exchanged clothes with the priest and Amphibalus made his escape in the guise of a Roman citizen, but Alban was arrested.

Yet so great was Alban's new found faith that he

desired earnestly to shed his blood for Christ. He was bound and led before the Judge who was, at that moment, offering sacrifice to his idols. He was furious that Alban's clever deception had allowed the priest to escape and quickly passed judgement: 'As you have concealed a sacrilegious man and blasphemer, and assisted in his escape from justice, you shall have his fate if you refuse to sacrifice to the gods.'

Alban replied that he could never obey such an order because he was a Christian and only worshipped the one true God, who had created all things.

'If you wish to continue to enjoy life, sacrifice!' thundered the Judge.

'The sacrifices you offer are made to devils,' Alban retorted.

'Whoever sacrifices to these idols shall receive their reward with the devils in hell.'

The Judge was enraged. He ordered that Alban be scourged, but seeing that Alban accepted it with courage and joy he eventually condemned him to be beheaded.

A mighty crowd went out to witness the execution, leaving the Judge alone in the city. There was a fast flowing river (almost certainly the River Ver) for all to cross before they could arrive at the place of execution, and so great was the crowd swarming across the bridge and slowing the passage of everyone that Alban, growing impatient to receive the crown of martyrdom, lifted up his eyes to heaven and prayed. Immediately, the waters of the river parted then dried up, allowing Alban and the multitude to pass safely over.

The executioner, astounded by this miracle and the saintly behaviour of Alban threw down his sword to be converted on the spot. This led to a delay in the proceedings for a new executioner to be found. Meanwhile Alban, followed by the crowd was led up to the top of a hill, a hill covered with all kinds of wild flowers, his place of execution and where an impressive cathedral now stands. There he fell down on his knees to offer his soul to God and as he prayed, a fountain sprang up for Alban to refresh himself.

A new executioner had been found and without hesitation he struck off the head of Alban. Miraculously, the executioner's eyes fell to the ground in a vivid manifestation of God's power and displeasure. The executioner who had thrown his sword away now declared himself to be a Christian and he also was beheaded, being baptised in his own blood.

Many of those who had witnessed the executions were also converted to the Christian faith and followed Amphibalus, the priest who had converted Alban, into Wales. Tragically, these new converts were later to be cut to pieces by idolaters, while the priest was brought back to be stoned to death at Radburn, three miles from St Albans.

The miracles surrounding St Alban would appear to be incredible, yet not so incredible as the actions and the faith of one holy man which led to the conversion and the heavenly reward of so many.

St Joan of Arc
(1412-1431)
May 30

The life of Joan of Arc and the complicated history of England and France are inextricably linked, particularly the traumatic years which preceded Joan's meteoric rise to fame, her triumph and tragic, lonely death.

When Edward III of England began to enforce his dubious claim to the throne of France, resulting in the Hundred Years War, he bequeathed a legacy of hatred. In 1415, Henry V renewed the claim and with his own outstanding abilities as a commander triumphing in the Battle of Agincourt, he became the master of Northern France. Henry introduced order and sound government, but on the French side Charles VI was mad and the Dauphin just a child. There were feuds within the French Royal Family and each faction was quite prepared to assist the invader in pursuit of their own ends.

Ever since 1407, the Houses of the Armagnacs and Burgundy had been at war with each other, with Burgundy receiving help from Henry in the form of money and military supplies. The death of Henry V changed little; his brother the Duke of Bedford continued to rule wisely and compassionately so the French people welcomed his just rule. Even Paris, though not under the English was strongly pro-English, so when Henry VI was crowned king it seemed likely he would rule over the two nations with little opposition, even though he was only ten years old.

Then Charles VI of France died and the accession of his son brought about feelings of strong patriotism. Charles VII was much more of a king than his father and the efforts of the French were concentrated on saving the city of Orleans, besieged by the English under the command of the Earl of Suffolk. It was a time of national crisis and help came from a surprising and totally unexpected quarter.

Joan of Arc had been born at the obscure village of Domremy, situated on the banks of the River Meuse; the daughter of James and Isobel Darc – deeply religious peasants. Joan did her share of ploughing and sowing, reaping and spinning, she looked after the animals and attended to domestic duties. A pious girl, she attended daily Mass, made visits to the Blessed Sacrament and always showed great charity to the poor.

The consequences of the terrible foreign invasion were brought home to the villagers of Domremy when they had to flee from the hands of marauding soldiers. On one occasion, the humble home of the Darcs was plundered then burnt to the ground. This traumatic experience, and the old prophesies that 'The fair realm of France' was to be redeemed from the English invaders by a woman, made a great impression on the little Joan. It soon became her constant meditation and the cause of all her fervent prayers.

In August 1424, the French and their traditional Scottish allies, led by the Duc de Tourraine, were heavily defeated at Verneuil by the Duke of Bedford and his deadly archers. It stunned the French but set Joan praying all the more. The following summer of 1425 she was at home, in the garden when: 'I heard a voice from God, for my help and guidance. The first time I heard this voice I was very much frightened, it came from the direction of the church... I believe it was sent to me from God. When I heard it for the third time, I recognised it was the voice of an angel.'

The 'voices' did not come alone, sometimes there were visions of angels, of St Michael the Archangel, St Catharine and St Margaret the long ago Queen of Scotland. The messages in the beginning bade her to be a good girl, to go often to church, to put her trust in God. Then an order came: She must leave her village and deliver Orleans.

Poor Joan was dumbfounded. How could she, a humble peasant girl ever hope to command those in highest authority, to lead soldiers into battle against the dreaded English? The mere idea of it was preposterous but the 'voices' continued more persistent than ever. She was no dreamer but a girl of remarkable common sense and she consulted with her uncle, Durant Laxard in whom she had great trust. At first he was sceptical but her persistence finally persuaded him and he took her to Vaucouleurs to see Robert de Baudricourt, the King's Commander, where she told him of the 'voices' and heavenly commands. At first she was ridiculed; all military commanders are accustomed to well-meaning individuals and cranks trying to tell them how to win the war, but in the end he listened. He gave her a letter to take to the Dauphin, to obtain an army and raise the siege of Orleans.

With Jean de Novelonpont, her two brothers and an escort, Joan found her way through the perilous territory of the Burgundians, the allies of the English, to reach

Chinon on 6 March. She delivered her message to the Dauphin in open court; prelates, courtiers, advisors and lawyers were won over by her faith and sincerity: the blessing was given to her mission. Joan, mounted on a black steed and clothed in shining armour led the way at the head of the army – to raise the siege of Orleans.

In her hand she carried a sacred sword which was found, according to her prophecy, under the altar of the Church of St Catharine de Furbois. She bore a white banner adorned with lilies and the legend: *Gesú, Maria* separated by a cross.

Joan and her army fought their way through the besieging English lines, even though battles in the past had proved that one English soldier was more than equal to four French. Amidst all the fighting, Joan was the inspiration of her troops even when she was severely wounded by an arrow. In the attack on the great English fort she told her troops: 'Wait till my banner touches the walls, then go in and all is yours.'

They did as she had ordered and soon they were the victors: the Siege of Orleans was raised on 9 May 1429. In the next campaign, victories again: at Jargean, Troyes, Beaugency and Chalons. She displayed the highest courage and enthusiasm but insisted upon decency and morality in all her men. This girl of eighteen showed herself to be a valiant leader with Napoleonic military qualities.

On 17 July 1429, the Dauphin was crowned king at Rheims. Her mission completed, she requested that she be allowed to return home. Her request was refused but she and her family were ennobled, honours which

Joan had never sought – only the satisfaction of fulfilling her sacred task of delivering France from the hands of the English.

Her life's work was accomplished, but disaster loomed. On 24 May 1430, Joan was captured by the Burgundians and after being imprisoned in the Castle of Beaulieu for four months, she was sold to the Duke of Bedford by John of Luxembourg for 10,000 livres.

This was not the age of chivalry. Insults and outrages were heaped on Joan by brutal soldiers, her sworn enemies; and as badly as she was treated, Charles VII of France, who owed everything to her, callously abandoned her to her fate. The English attributed her wonderful success in battle to sorcery. As a prisoner of war she could not be legally punished but as she was deemed to be a witch, well, that was a different matter.

The vile Pierre Cauchon, the Bishop of Beauvais and a court of fifty ecclesiastics and lawyers – all of them the Duke of Bedford's men – tried Joan on 21 February 1431. Alone and unaided she faced her judges and maintained her mission was a call from God. The trial lasted until 23 May. She was condemned as a relapsed heretic and burned to death in the Market Place at Rouen, 30 May 1431.

'My voices were from God,' declared the dying heroine; in death as in life, she was true to her sacred cause.

Twenty-four years after this despicable crime against a nineteen-year-old girl, Pope Calistus III had the whole process investigated and the trial and condemnation of Joan of Arc was declared to be a disgraceful miscarriage of justice. Belief in her sanctity grew, and spread from France to all over the Catholic world.

But what, precisely, did Joan's mission accomplish? At the time, the prospect of good and settled government held out a possibility of long English rule under which the French people themselves would enjoy the blessings of peace, order and justice.

But if France *had* come under the rule of the English, then in the following century the Tudors who laid waste the Catholic Church in England would have certainly done exactly the same in France; then France and maybe the whole of Europe would have been lost to the Faith. Instead, in the dark days of penal times in England, France, saved from the English by Joan of Arc, was a powerhouse of the Faith.

Indeed, God works in strange ways!

St Januarius
(AD 305)
September 19

Januarius was the Bishop of Benevento, Italy, when the persecutions of Diocletian erupted. The deacons Sosius and Proculus and the eminent laymen Eutyches and Acutius were arrested and imprisoned for the faith at Puzzuoli by the order of Dracontius, the governor of Campania.

When Januarius went to comfort his friend Sosius and their fellow Christians in prison, the visit of such a distinguished man did not go unnoticed by the jailers and Timothy, who had succeeded Dracontius as governor was informed. He gave orders that Bishop Januarius should be arrested and brought before him at his residence at Nola. Festus a deacon and Desiderius a lector were also arrested.

They were all interrogated, tortured and when the governor later travelled to Fuzzuoli, Januarius and his companions were loaded with heavy chains and made to walk in front of the governor's chariot to the town. There they were thrown into prison with Sosius and the others and all of them were condemned by order of the Emperor to be thrown to the wild beasts.

The sentence was carried out in the amphitheatre yet, to the amazement of the crowd, the beasts could not be provoked into killing Januarius and the other holy men, so they were beheaded. The sentence was carried out at Puzzuoli and there they were buried.

In about 400, when the persecutions had ceased, the remains of these holy martyrs were rescued by their fellow Christians, and the relics of St Januarius taken to Naples. During the wars of the Normans they were transferred to Benevento, then to the abbey of Monte Vergine and back to Naples in 1497 for St Januarius to become the principal patron of the city. Over the centuries the eruptions of Mount Vesuvius have constantly threatened the city, but the intercession of the saint was always implored and Naples was spared.

In a chapel called the Treasury, in the Cathedral of Naples the blood of St Januarius, dark and congealed, is sealed in two very old glass vials. Yet on the saint's feast day and other public occasions in the year when the vials are brought to the saint's head (encased in a silver bust) the congealed blood becomes liquid and froths and bubbles into a bright, ruby red. Despite numerous attempts by incredulous scientists to interpret this phenomenon, no satisfactory explanation has yet been found.

This manifestation has been taking place ever since the first translation of the saint's relics in the year 400.

St Stephen the first Martyr
(AD 35)
December 26

In the years following the crucifixion of Jesus and the descent of the Holy Spirit on the Apostles, the numbers of converts to the faith increased dramatically. The new converts lived together, loving one another as true brethren and supporting and encouraging one another by prayer and material help under the guidance of the Apostles. But as the numbers grew, more help was needed for their overall care. So seventy-two disciples were chosen and from these seven deacons were appointed: Stephen, Philip, Prochorus, Nicanor, Timon, Parmenas and Nicholas. As Peter was first among the Apostles, so Stephen was first among the deacons and called Archdeacon, 'a man full of faith and the Holy Spirit'.

Stephen preached the Gospel with undaunted courage and inspired zeal, confirming his doctrine by many public and unquestionable miracles. But the success of this holy deacon stirred up malice and envy in the hearts of the enemies of the faith and they began to dispute with Stephen. They were unsuccessful in their denunciations, quite unable to resist the wisdom and the spirit with which he spoke, so they concocted false charges of his blasphemy against Moses and against God.

The charges were laid against him in the Sanhedrin and Caiphas the high priest ordered him to make his defence. Stephen showed that Moses had foretold a new law and the Messiah. He acknowledged that Solomon had built the Temple, but declared that the Temple and the Law of Moses were temporary institutions that were to give way to Christianity founded by Jesus Christ, the Messiah sent by God. Yet just as their ancestors had persecuted and slain many of the prophets who had foretold the coming of the Christ, so they had crucified him.

This stinging reproach enraged his persecutors; voices were raised in anger, fists were shaken and pointing fingers condemned. Stephen's face was the face of an angel as he raised his eyes and saw the heavens open above him. This vision inspired Stephen with new courage, his heart and soul overflowing in joy and in ecstasy. Unable to contain such happiness even in the midst of his tormentors he declared: 'Behold, I see the heavens open before me and the Son of man standing at the right hand of the Father.'

The rage of the Jews boiled over into murderous intent when they heard Stephen's bold declaration. They condemned him as a blasphemer, and in a fury of blind zeal they didn't wait for official condemnation but dragged him out of the city to stone him without mercy.

As the blows fell, Stephen prayed: 'Lord Jesus, receive my soul.'

Falling to his knees he cried out: 'Lord, lay not this sin to their charge.'

In a torrent of stones he fell asleep in the Lord, the death of the just, his rest after the toils of this painful life.

A small, bandy-legged official held the clothes of

those who stoned him, encouraging them in their grisly work and believing he was an agent in the works of God. It was only later that he realised his great mistake, when he was on the road to Damascus and heard the words, 'Saul, Saul, why do you persecute me?' And the persecutor of the Christians became Paul, the great Apostle of the Gentiles.

The body of the martyr was left exposed for a day and a night yet it remained untouched by wild beasts or birds of prey. Later, at the instigation of the holy man Gamaliel (whose wisdom had prevailed at the trial of St Peter) the remains of Stephen were taken by the Christians and buried... to be discovered almost four hundred years later in a most amazing fashion.

The exact location of the burial place of the martyr had long ago faded into memory but in 415 Lucian, a venerable priest of a church called Caphargamala had a vision. He was sleeping in the baptistery when, half awake, he saw a tall old man with a long white beard, clothed in a white garment and holding a golden wand in his hand. He called Lucian three times by name, then told him to go to Jerusalem and tell Bishop John to come and open the tombs in which his remains and that of other devout servants of God lay.

Lucian was perplexed, but he asked his name. 'I am Gamaliel who instructed Paul the Apostle in the law,' he replied. 'In the tombs you will find Stephen who was stoned by the Jews, Nicodemus who came to Jesus by night, my beloved son Abibas who died at the age of twenty and the body of myself.'

Lucian didn't really know what to think. Was it just a dream, was this old man a fiendish impostor? He prayed that if the vision was from God he might see it at least three times, in the meantime continuing to fast on bread and water. On the following Friday, Gamaliel again appeared commanding him to obey and he showed Lucian four baskets, three of gold and one of silver. The golden baskets were filled with roses, two of white and one of red, the silver basket was full of sweet-smelling saffron. Lucian asked what they meant.

Gamaliel replied, 'These are our relics. The red roses represent Stephen, the silver basket is for my son who departed this life without stain. The others are Nicodemus and myself.'

A third time Gamaliel appeared and again commanded him to go to the bishop, that the tombs would be opened, adding that the great drought which had afflicted the whole country would only be lifted when the relics were revealed.

Lucian, by now terrified, went to Jerusalem to reveal the visions to Bishop John. The bishop was overjoyed and instructed Lucian to search for the tombs under a heap of stones near to his church. With the help of the local people Lucian searched and found nothing, but a holy monk named Migetus informed him that the holy man Gamaliel had appeared to him and he was to tell Lucian the priest to search at a place called Debatalia.

After digging there, three coffins were discovered. They were boldly inscribed: Cheliel, Nasuam, Gamaliel and Abibas. The first two were the Syrian names of Stephen and Nicodemus. Upon opening Stephen's coffin, the earth shook and an incredible perfumed odour enveloped the vast multitude assembled there, many of whom were sick with a variety of diseases.

Seventy-three of them were cured on the spot. The holy relics were venerated and the tombs closed.

The coffin of Stephen was carried in procession to the church of Sion in Jerusalem, during which the rains came and the drought was over. The remains of St Stephen finally came to rest in a church built in his honour close to the place where he was stoned to death, erected in the year 444 by the Empress Eudocia, the wife of Theodosius the Younger.

In the long line of glorious martyrs someone had to be the first; that honour fell to Stephen and so he became known as 'The first martyr'.

St Thomas More

(1478-1535)

July 6

The fate of St Thomas More could be considered as a challenge to all who hold public office. Would they be prepared, like him, to abandon fame and fortune, to sacrifice the king's friendship and one of the most powerful positions in the land? To willingly accept a cruel death for the sake of honest principles and, above all, the faith? And in doing so leave behind family and friends?

The son of a London judge, he was born at Milk Street in Cheapside, London, on 7 February 1478. It is recorded that just before his birth his mother saw a vision of her son 'bright with splendour'.

His education began at St Anthony's School in Threadneedle Street then afterwards he went as page of honour to Cardinal Morton, Archbishop of Canterbury. It was then to Oxford and in 1494 More entered the legal profession, as a student at Lincoln's Inn. He studied hard, lectured at Furneval's Inn and became a young barrister, yet despite his worldly success he was deeply religious and seriously considered joining the Carthusians. After considerable prayer and contemplation he decided a religious vocation was not for him but a vocation of another kind; in 1505 he married Jane Colt. It was a happy union with three daughters and one son, yet it ended in sadness when Jane died in 1511. Shortly afterwards

More was married again, to Alice Middleton. She was seven years his senior and proved to be an excellent wife and caring stepmother.

More's ascent to the pinnacles of public life was rapid. As a barrister, his practice rewarded him with an extremely handsome salary; he became under-sheriff of London and at the age of twenty-six he was elected to Parliament. More was rich, a renowned public figure, but privately he dedicated himself to his family and to the Christian education of his children. He went on pilgrimages whenever possible and never hoarded money but gave it away to the destitute and the sick. He slept just four or five hours a night, constantly wore a hair shirt and attended mass when he was able. He was blessed with a happy and carefree, yet inflexible temperament and this had been revealed in 1505 when, as a Member of Parliament, he had successfully opposed a grant of £113,000 requested by the King, Henry VII, for the marriage of his daughter Margaret to James IV, King of Scotland.

In 1509 Henry VII died, to be succeeded by his son, the young and later notorious Henry VIII. More's career continued in the ascendancy; by 1515 he was Sheriff of London and had travelled extensively on the continent, and then in 1516 he published his *Utopia*, a work concerning the ideal social and political system.

In 1520 he accompanied Henry to his meeting with Francis I of France at the Field of the Cloth of Gold near Calais, set up by Cardinal Wolsey in an attempt to increase English influence in Europe. The year following he was appointed Under Treasurer of England and in 1523 he became Speaker of the House of

Commons. It was at this time he moved house to Chelsea to better accommodate his large, happy, intellectual family. Here always it was open house; for the king often called to walk in the gardens with More, his great friend and the wisest man in the kingdom. They had much in common; each was young and powerful, combining a great zest for life with a devout love for the Catholic Church.

But Henry had a problem which mounted with the passing of time. His marriage to Catherine of Aragon had produced no male heir, so he eventually decided to seek an annulment from Rome and then marry Anne Boleyn. Cardinal Wolsey, the Lord Chancellor, a man who had used his position to amass great wealth and so bring the Church into disrepute, failed in his negotiations on Henry's behalf with Rome. The Pope refused the request for an annulment and Henry was furious. Wolsey was dismissed and replaced by Thomas More.

The king then acted ruthlessly and decisively. The wheels of intimidation were set into motion for Parliament to pass a new succession law and proclaim Henry head of the Church of England.

More resigned his Chancellorship in protest, then prepared himself and his family for the worst. His resignation enraged the king who he felt that it was a severe and public censure on his conduct. Vile charges of corruption while in office were made against More, with other surreptitious moves made to discredit him, and there were subtle efforts to make it look as if he *had* actually taken the oath. His wife and daughter pleaded with him but More rejected all compromise.

But the king had a master card to play and he knew it was a winner: take the oath or else. And More fully understood what *that* meant.

He could, like so many of his fellow statesmen have acquiesced and swallowed his principles, abandoned his faith and so retained his fame and position, but he didn't. He refused to take the oath and so he was imprisoned in the Tower of London. And it was from his cell window on 8 May 1535 that he watched, with a prayer on his lips and admiration in his heart as the Carthusian Martyrs were dragged away on hurdles to the ultimate sacrifice at Tyburn. Their bravery was a profound example for him: the Grace of God would sustain him.

At his so-called trial in Westminster Hall he appeared old and totally worn out; illness and imprisonment had taken their toll yet he easily disproved the charges brought against him. But his eloquence made no difference; the court was heavily loaded against him and he was sentenced to death.

He was beheaded on Tower Hill on the morning of 6 July 1535, declaring that he died for the sake of the Catholic Church and adding: 'I am the king's good servant, but God's first.'

St Helen

(AD 326)

August 18

St Helen has two quite enormous claims to fame: she was the mother of Constantine the Great and she discovered the true Cross of Christ. The only daughter of King Coilus (who gave his name to the city of Colchester) she married Constantius, an officer in the Roman army. She bore him a son, Constantine, then in the year 293 Constantius was proclaimed Caesar. He left Helen to marry the step-daughter of Emperor Maximian, ruled over the Roman Empire for fourteen years and died in 306.

Then Helen's fortunes changed. Her son's troops proclaimed him Caesar and in 312 he defeated his enemies at the Battle of Milvian Bridge after invoking the help of the one, true God and being inspired by miraculous visions. He entered Rome victorious, declared in favour of Christianity and conferred the title of 'Empress' on his mother. At the age of sixty-three Helen became a Christian and with the encouragement of her son she built churches, assisted orphans and widows and contributed enormous amounts of money to the poor. Even though she was mistress of the Empire, Helen attended Mass as a humble member of the congregation to worship with incomparable faith and zeal.

But in the East, the Empire of Constantine was under threat from the armies of Lucinius who promised that if his gods gave him victory he would exterminate their enemies. Constantine prepared himself for battle by fasting and prayer, and ordered that the ensign of the Cross be carried before his army. Despite being considerably outnumbered, Constantine defeated Lucinius at Adrianople in July 324, leaving 30,000 dead. In a second battle near Chalcidon only 3,000 of his enemies escaped out of an army of 130,000 men. Lucinius was captured yet Constantine spared his life to send him into exile in Greece, but after hearing that Lucinius was making preparations to march again, Constantine ordered him to be strangled.

Constantine was now the master of the East. In 326 he wrote to Macarius, the Bishop of Jerusalem declaring his desire to build a magnificent church on Mount Calvary. His mother Helen, though eighty years of age undertook the task of seeing this pious work executed, and she decided at the same time that she would seek the sacred cross on which Christ had died. She consulted with anyone and everyone who could help her in her search, and Helen was reliably informed that if she could find the sepulchre of Christ she would most likely find the instruments of punishment, as it was the custom of the Jews to bury these detestable objects out of sight but close to the place of burial.

The Emperor Hadrian had built a temple to Venus over the site, Helen ordered it to be pulled down and the profane rubbish removed. Then, after digging to a great depth the holy sepulchre was discovered and close by three wooden crosses, together with nails and the title which had been fixed to the Saviour's Cross. Unfortunately this was lying loose, so which was the true Cross?

Bishop Macarius had an idea. He knew that a certain lady in the city was extremely ill, so he suggested to Helen that the three crosses be taken to her. This was done and the Bishop prayed that God would reward their faith. Each cross was laid on the lady and she recovered immediately at the touch of the true cross.

Helen was overjoyed. She built a magnificent church on the hallowed spot, the true cross displayed in a rich case of silver. Chips of the precious wood were cut daily from the cross by devout people yet it suffered no diminution, a miracle comparable to the feeding of the five thousand. The holy Empress afterwards took a part of the cross to her son, the Emperor Constantine, then in Constantinople, who received it with joy and great veneration. Another part she carried to Rome to be later placed in a church specially built for it: the Church of the Holy Cross of Jerusalem.

Her life's work completed, Helen died in the arms of her devoted son on 18 August, in the year of Our Lord 326.

St Peter, the first Pope
(AD 65)
June 29

'You are Peter, and upon this rock I will build my church, and the powers of death shall not prevail against it. And I will give you the keys of the kingdom of heaven. And whatever you bind on earth, shall be bound in heaven; and whatever you loose on earth shall be loosed also in heaven.'

With these words, Jesus appointed Peter as his successor as the head of his church, the church he promised 'to be with all days, even to the consummation of the world'.

Peter was originally called Simon until Jesus gave him his new name signifying 'Rock'. He was the son of Jonas and the brother of St Andrew, who first introduced him to Jesus. When he was young, Peter lived in Bethsaida in Galilee, and like his brother he was a fisherman. After his marriage he moved to Capharnaum, probably because his wife's mother lived there. The brothers had always lived in expectation of the Messiah, and Andrew became a disciple of John the Baptist who many thought to be the Messiah, as did Peter.

But after Andrew had met Jesus he was convinced he had found the true Messiah. He told Peter, and his brother believed even though he had not yet met Jesus. When eventually they did meet, Jesus gave him his new name. They returned to fishing but at the end of that year, the first in the ministry of Jesus, while they were washing their nets, Jesus went out in Peter's boat to preach to the multitude gathered on the shore. When Jesus had finished preaching he told Peter to cast his net into the sea. Peter and the others had fished all night and caught nothing, but in obedience he let down his net – his boat was swamped by the miraculous draught of fishes.

Peter was amazed. He fell down on his knees in humility before Jesus to cry out, 'Depart from me, O Lord, for I am a sinful man.'

Jesus said to Peter, 'Fear not, henceforth thou shalt catch people.'

When they had brought their boats back to land they left all things and followed him. By this miracle Jesus gave them a foretaste of their future success as his followers and the eternal happiness in the world to come. Soon after this, Jesus cured Peter's mother-in-law of a fever.

In the year 31, Jesus chose his twelve Apostles and right from the beginning Peter took the chief place among them. When weak disciples deserted, Jesus asked the twelve, 'Would you also go away?' It was Peter who answered, 'Lord, to whom shall we go? You have the words of eternal life.' So he acknowledged his love for his Lord and his Master.

At the transfiguration it was Peter who spoke, 'Lord, it is good for us to be here.'

When the Apostles were in the boat crossing the sea, Jesus came from the shore walking on the water. Peter begged that he should come to meet him but when he stepped on the waves, fear weakened his confidence and he began to sink. Then Jesus took his hand to save him. This incident shows us what we can do, even in seemingly impossible situations, when God is with us.

When Jesus offered to wash the feet of Peter at the Last Supper he cried out in surprise and humility, 'Lord, do you wash my feet? You shall never wash my feet!' Then terrified that he would otherwise be excluded he fervently agreed.

His protestation that he would die for Jesus was because of his confidence in his own courage and strength of resolution, yet a distrust of ourselves is essential for true humility. To curb this rising presumption, Jesus foretold that he would deny him three times. And he did.

Yet the love of Jesus for Peter was shown when he witnessed the transfiguration with James and John. Jesus took the same three Apostles with him to the garden of Gethsemane, to be close to them in his agony and bloody sweat. When Judas arrived with the Jews to seize Jesus it was Peter who tried to defend his Master when he drew his sword to cut off the ear of Malchus. It was after this that Peter denied Jesus; at the third denial Jesus turned to look at him... and Peter wept. And, it is said, his cheeks became furrowed by the streams of tears.

After the resurrection it was Peter who first entered the tomb. Jesus appeared to Mary Magdalen and then on the same day to Peter. Some days later when Peter was fishing on the lake of Tiberias he saw Jesus on the shore, and he jumped into the water to swim ashore to meet the Lord. There, Jesus had a meal of broiled fish and bread waiting and Jesus ate with them, proving he was not a ghost but totally alive. After they had eaten, Jesus asked Peter three times if he loved him more than the rest of the disciples. Peter told him that he *knew* his love was most sincere, yet he was troubled to be asked three times. But this was to expiate the three times he had denied Jesus.

Jesus appeared to the Apostles assembled on a mountain in Galilee and there he gave them a commission to preach the Gospel to all nations, promising to be with his Church till the end of time. So these poor illiterate men were made the instruments of this great work, and at their head was an ignorant fisherman. Yet this little band triumphed over the wisdom of philosophers, the eloquence of orators, the authority of kings and the passions of men. The Spirit of God was powerful in their understanding and speech; the evidence of their testimony was confirmed by innumerable and uncontested miracles; the heavenly sanctity of their words and actions was sealed eventually by the blood of martyrdom.

These extraordinary gifts and graces came from the descent of the Holy Spirit upon them. Peter, in a sermon to the Jews converted over three thousand! With the Apostle John he was entering the Temple by way of the Beautiful Gate when he saw a lame man begging for alms. Peter commanded him in the name of Jesus Christ to rise up and walk... and the man found he was perfectly healed. After this miracle Peter gave a second sermon to the people and five thousand were converted.

The priests and Sadducees were alarmed at this success, and Peter and John were arrested and imprisoned. The court of Annas and Caiaphas found no charge proved against them so they were released and warned not to preach again in the name of Jesus. Peter replied: 'Whether it be just to obey you or rather God, be yourselves the judges.'

The new Christians lived in a spirit of common good, sharing all their worldly goods, but in the heart of Annanias and his wife Sapphira there lurked the vice of avarice. Pretending to give away all their possessions, they had secretly retained a part for themselves. Peter, to whom God had revealed their hypocrisy reproached them and at his severe reprimand Annanias and his wife fell dead at his feet.

The Apostles confirmed their doctrine by many miracles; Caiaphas was incensed and once again Peter was in prison. But the chains binding his hands and feet fell away in the night and an angel guided him to freedom. The next day Peter and the Apostles were once again preaching in the temple. Arrested again, they were interrogated, but the wisdom of Gamaliel, a renowned doctor of law prevailed. He advised the court to wait and see, to consider whether the doctrine of the Apostles, confirmed by miracles, came from God or not. If it *was* from God they could do nothing about it. If it was *not* from God it would simply die away. However, the Apostles were scourged but went away rejoicing. This, their spirit, was the greatest of all miracles.

The persecutions of the Christians dying down, Peter visited the faithful in other countries. At Lydda he cured a man who was sick of the palsy and at Joppa he raised to life the widow Tabitha. By the order of an angel he baptised Cornelius, a centurion and a Gentile, and on this occasion God showed him in a vision the call of the Gentiles to the faith.

About this time the Apostles dispersed to preach the Gospel. Peter was destined to carry the word of God to Rome, the capital city of the Roman Empire and the world. Yet Peter made many visits to various countries to spread the faith: he was in Jerusalem in 37 when Paul paid him a visit, and he preached widely in the East before he went to Rome to make it the chief place of his labours. It was also a city of iniquity and Peter realised that by triumphing in Rome he would open the way to conquering the world for Christ. A rash enterprise for an ignorant fisherman; the humility of Calvary and the ignominy of the Cross were hardly suited to the pride and splendour and pomp of the capital.

He preached to the Jews and the Gentiles, formed a Church composed of both and held the see of Rome for twenty-five years, though he was often in other countries where he established bishops. He wrote two canonical epistles while in Rome and it is a tradition there that he converted the house of Pudens, a Roman senator, into a church which now bears the name of St Peter's.

The magician Simon Magus had great influence in the court of Rome. On one occasion he promised the Emperor and the people that he would fly in the air, carried by his angels in imitation of the ascension of Christ. Peter and Paul watching the illusion prayed, Simon Magus fell to the ground, broke a leg and died a few days later.

The faith continued to gain strength in Rome by the miracles and the preaching of the Apostles, so in 64 the Emperor Nero started a great persecution against the Church. The Christians urged Peter to flee to safety and though unwilling to do so, one night he did. But going out of a gate of the city he met Jesus Christ. Peter asked the immortal question: '*Quo vadis*?' Where are you going? Jesus answered, 'I am going to Rome to be crucified again.'

Peter understood. It was the will of God that he should suffer, so he returned to the city to be taken and put into the Mamertine prison with Paul. There they remained for eight months and during this time they converted Processus and Martinian, the captains of their guard, together with forty-seven others.

Peter and Paul were scourged before being put to death and together they were led out of the city by the Ostian Gate, to suffer in a field on the banks of the River Tiber. As a Roman citizen, Paul was beheaded. Peter requested that he be crucified head down, saying that he was not worthy to die in the manner of his Saviour. The executioners readily granted this amazing request, so he was bound with ropes and nailed to his cross. The bodies were buried in the catacombs two miles outside Rome.

Here they remained for eighteen months. The body of St Paul was taken to the Ostian Way, the body of St Peter to the Vatican Hill. The heads of the saints are at present kept in silver bustoes in the Church of St John Lateran.

St Peter left all things to follow Jesus Christ and in return he received from him the promise of life everlasting. He earned the love and respect and awesome admiration of all the faithful.

St Paul

(AD 65)

June 30

The events leading up to Paul's martyrdom in Rome had begun many years earlier on the road to Damascus. Saul, as was originally known, was a stern and unremitting disciple of the Mosaic Law and he regarded the emerging Christians, the followers of the crucified Jesus as enemies of the Law of God – not realising that Jesus had come to fulfil the Mosaic Law, not to destroy it.

A tent-maker by trade, Saul, with the official blessing of the high priest was on his way to Damascus to seek and capture any Christians he could find. He had already enthusiastically assisted at the stoning of St Stephen. But as he was travelling on that road, probably the most spectacular conversion ever took place. A bright celestial light shone down from heaven and as Saul fell to the ground he heard a voice saying, 'Saul, Saul, why do you persecute me?'

'Who are you, Lord?' Saul asked.

'I am Jesus who you are persecuting,' said the voice. 'But rise and enter the city, and you will be told what you are to do.'

Saul's cohorts had observed it all in dumb amazement; they had heard a voice yet there was no one to be seen. Now Saul could not see them; he had been struck blind.

They led him by the hand into Damascus, to a house

in a street called 'Strait' and here he stayed for three days, neither eating nor drinking. Then Ananias came, sent by Jesus. The disciple laid hands on him, Saul immediately regained his sight and then he was baptised.

Filled with the Holy Spirit, Saul at once began preaching the word of Jesus, much to the astonishment of the people to whom he was the scourge of the Christians. The Jews branded Saul a traitor and planned to kill him, but Saul's friends let him down from the city wall in a basket and so he escaped. He took the opportunity to visit Peter in Jerusalem.

It was Barnabas who convinced the Apostles of Saul's conversion and sincerity. Understandably, many of the Christians were apprehensive in view of Saul's past persecutions against them, but he was accepted, and his apostleship began.

For three years he laboured in Tarsus, his own city, and in Cilicia and Syria. It was at this time, about the year 44, that Saul was granted an ecstasy in which he was taken up to heaven and there saw and heard sublime mysteries. He was afterwards humiliated with a 'sting of the flesh' and attacks from Satan; Saul responded with fasting and other mortifications.

He travelled with Barnabas to Antioch, sailed to Cyprus and preached at Paphos. Elymas, a sorcerer opposed him and Saul struck him blind. (He was later to recover his sight when he became a Christian.) While in Cyprus, Saul converted Sergius Paulus, the Roman proconsul, a much respected and illustrious man and it is said that Saul took the name of Paul from him. From Cyprus it was by sea to Pamphilia then back to Antioch where many were converted by Paul's fiery eloquence. He feared no dangers or difficulties and neither was he daunted by threats of death – so fierce was his love for God he delighted in the greatest sufferings; so immense that he could truly say that he carried the wounds of Christ in his own body.

Yet hostile and obstinate Jews drove them out of Antioch, leaving Paul bruised and battered. Next it was to Iconium and then to Lystra, where Paul cured a man who had been lame from birth. The heathens were much impressed and thought that Barnabas was Jupiter and Paul, Mercury; but when they refused the honour of being 'gods', the crowd was upset and Paul was badly beaten and left half dead. So they returned to Antioch having been away for three years.

Over the next four years Paul preached throughout Syria and Judea and went to Jerusalem for the first general council held by the Apostles. He visited the churches he had founded, but when he was in Troas, he saw in a vision a Macedonian pleading with him to come to his country, so Paul sailed to Samothracia with Silas, Luke and Timothy. They went to the eminent church at Phillipi and one day on the road Paul cured a young girl who was possessed by the devil. Due to a complaint by the masters of the girl who had lost a money-making freak they found themselves in prison.

That night, manacled in their cell, an earthquake shook the prison. Doors flew open, their manacles fell to the ground and the jailer, assuming his prisoners had all escaped, prepared to lean on his sword. A cry from Paul stopped him, and he convinced the jailer that they had not escaped. As a result, the jailer and all his household were baptised.

They left Phillipi for Thessalonica only for the house where they were staying to be attacked by hostile Jews, but Paul and Silas were hidden by the Christians and they escaped in the night. In Athens, the Holy Spirit inspired Paul to go to Corinth and here he plied his trade as a tent-maker while preaching in the synagogue on the Sabbath. It was from here that he wrote his first epistle – to the Thessalonians, about the year 52.

Over the next three years he travelled through Galatia, Phrygia, parts of Asia, from Cappadocia to Ephesus and he then returned to Troas. Here, while Paul was preaching in the third storey room of a house, a young man fell asleep during the lengthy discourse, and tumbled right down to the ground, dead. Paul restored him to life, and carried on preaching until the dawn of the following day.

In 58 Paul made his fifth visit to Jerusalem. Here, the Jews accused him of defiling the temple and once again he was reviled and attacked. He was saved from imminent death with the arrival of Claudius Lysias, a Roman tribune and his men; nevertheless, he was put in chains. Lysias suspected he was a certain seditious Egyptian and ordered him to be scourged. Paul stated that as a Roman citizen he could not be whipped and Lysias, realising his mistake and afraid of the consequences released Paul.

Yet Paul was continually harassed by the Jews who still regarded him as a traitor, and again he was apprehended and brought before Festus, the governor of Judea. As a Roman citizen, Paul appealed to the

Emperor, so Festus had no alternative but to dispatch him to Rome, and this duty he delegated to Julius, a centurion, and a company of his men. So Paul, with Luke, Aristanchus and some others boarded a ship and sailed for the port of Mysia. They changed ship at Alexandria but due to contrary winds they sailed too far West and were wrecked in a violent storm on the island of Malta. Yet the prayers of Paul had been heard and all of the two hundred and seventy-two passengers survived.

In this far flung province of Rome the passengers were treated kindly, the inhabitants making huge fires for them to dry their clothes. As Paul threw a bundle of sticks on to a fire a viper bit into his hands but he shook it off and into the fire. Everyone expected that very soon Paul would swell up and die, but when it became clear he was unharmed they were sure he must be some kind of god. Publius, the Roman governor treated them all with great generosity and received his reward when Paul restored his father to health. After a stay of three months on the island they once again set off for Rome.

In the spring of 61 they arrived in the city where Julius delivered Paul into the hands of the Praefectus Praetorio. Paul was treated quite liberally and, with no accusers appearing against him he was eventually released. It was at this time that he wrote his epistles to the Philippians, before returning to the East to renew his preaching, suffering over again in chains, prisons, torments, conflicts and the ever present danger of death. Preaching to Jew or Gentile, to anyone who would listen.

He established the faith in Crete, leaving Titus as bishop there, as he did Timothy at Ephesus. Paul went back into Asia, returned to the East then it was to Rome, knowing from a revelation that he should suffer martyrdom in that city. He converted, among others, a favourite concubine of the Emperor Nero who changed her way of life completely to become a virtuous lady, but the emperor was enraged and Paul found himself once again in the Mamertine Prison. Yet from here he converted the cup bearer to the emperor, which incensed the tyrant more than ever.

Eloquent in Greek and Latin and next to John the evangelist, the greatest religious genius the Church has ever known, Paul's fourteen apostolic writings to the churches he had founded remain a fountain of faith to this day. During his life, this 'Apostle of the Gentiles', this man of miracles and mortification had been scourged five times by the Jews, three times beaten with rods and shipwrecked on three occasions. In his many travels it would seem that he had left a spiritual footprint in almost every corner of the known world.

Now at last he knew the end for him was near; he had run the race and the prize of eternal life was within his grasp – the Holy Spirit had already revealed this to him, even the day and the hour. His companion in death would be Peter, the earthly successor of his beloved Jesus, and their names would forever be inseparable in the calendar of the Saints. As a Roman citizen, Paul was spared the indignity of a crucifixion – he would die by the sword. It was 29 June AD 65.

Originally, the feasts of St Peter and St Paul were celebrated on the same day, 29 June, but as the festivities were found to be too exhausting and overwhelming by the church authorities, the feast of St Paul was transferred to 30 June.

The Japanese Martyrs
(1597-1647)
February 5

The mission of St Francis Xavier to convert the Japanese in the mid sixteenth century began to bear fruit almost immediately, a tribute to inspired missionary zeal but due in no small part to the prevailing feudal system. Within two years three thousand converts had been made to the Catholic Faith.

Fr Torres and other Jesuits continued the work so that by the year 1582 the number of converts had risen to 200,000. In 1592 it was 300,000. The success was unprecedented but all of this was suddenly to change.

In the year 1596, the *San Felipe*, a Spanish vessel carrying Brother Phillip (the future St Phillip of Jesus) and his companions was wrecked off the coast of Japan. They and the captain and crew were taken before the governor of the province and a tense state of affairs developed when cannon and ammunition were discovered among the wreckage of the vessel.

The captain and crew foolishly boasted of the power of the King of Spain, of what he could do and what he was about to do against their country. The authorities took these remarks very seriously, as the captain had intimated that the missionaries already in Japan were the advance guard of an army of invasion. They were all promptly thrown into prison and after some months transported to Nagasaki. Brother Phillip and his companions were called upon to renounce the Catholic

Faith, but all of them refused and all of them were condemned to death. They were martyred, Japanese style, with each of them hung up on a wooden cross and pierced with lances.

Some resentment against the missionaries had already been fermented by Buddhist priests and now that resentment turned into open persecution. In 1597, three Jesuits and twenty-six Franciscans suffered death, together with a number of native Christians. They were martyred at Nagasaki on 5 February, with cross and lance in the same way as St Phillip of Jesus and his companions.

For fifteen years the persecution ceased, then in 1616, by a decree of the Emperor Hedilada it burst forth again with a savagery not seen since the reign of Diocletion in the early days of the Church. On 22 September 1622, twenty-seven Christians were publicly beheaded and twenty-five more burned alive at Nagasaki. The same fate was to befall many other Christians in various parts of the empire.

In 1631 four thousand Christians were drowned at sea. The years 1642 and 1643 saw ten Spanish missionaries massacred after suffering inhuman tortures and in 1647 the same fate befell a band of religious. Christians were hunted with a price on their heads and the Japanese people were exhorted to trample publicly on a crucifix, all in an attempt to exterminate the Church.

For two hundred years Japan was isolated from the rest of the world except for business with a few Dutch traders, and so things remained until the year 1856 when a treaty was signed between France and Japan.

One of the terms of this treaty was that Christians would again be allowed into the ports of the country.

Evangelisation began all over again, and to the amazement of Père Petitjean and his colleagues of the Society of Foreign Missions, a total of fifty-thousand Christians were discovered in the country. A holy tribute to the steadfast faith of those converts who for almost two hundred and fifty years had been without pastoral care.

St Antony, Patriarch of Monks
(AD 356)
January 17

The year 276 saw the death of Antony's parents and not yet twenty years old, he found himself to be a very rich young man. Born at Coma, a village in Egypt, he was alone in the world and responsible for his younger sister. Six months later he was in a church when he heard the words of Christ to the rich young man read out: 'Go, sell what you have and give it to the poor'.

Antony took these words very much to heart. From his estate he made provision for himself and his sister regarding public taxes; the rest he gave to the poor. In a church he again listened as other words of Christ were read: 'Be not solicitous for tomorrow'. He acted upon these words immediately. He distributed in alms the money and goods he had reserved for himself, placed his sister in a convent and retired to be a hermit in a lonely place near his village. After a time, the devil began to assault him with a variety of crude temptations but Antony repulsed these attacks on his soul with the weapons of fasting, humility and constant prayer. The devil appeared in visible form as a young woman to tempt him, then as a black boy to terrify him, but the young novice triumphed.

Antony existed solely on bread, salt and water, never eating before sunset and only then every two or three days. To find a more remote solitude he moved further away from Coma to abide in an old sepulchre on a mountain, where a friend from time to time brought him a little bread. But Satan was to assault him again, to terrify him with dreadful noises and to beat him so harshly that he was covered in cuts and bruises and close to death. It was in this condition that he was found by his friend.

When he eventually began to recover, though not yet able to stand on his feet he cried out to the devil: 'Behold, I am here. Do your worst but nothing will ever separate me from Christ my Lord.'

The fiends appeared again in the guise of hideous beasts in an attempt to terrify him, till a ray of heavenly light appeared to chase them away. Antony cried out: 'Where were you my Lord and Master at the beginning of my conflict?'

A voice answered: 'Antony, I was here the whole time and watched you in combat. Because you withstood the enemy, I will forever protect you and make your name famous throughout the world.'

At these words Antony stood up, elated and strengthened, to pray and give thanks to his deliverer.

In about 305, Antony came down from his mountain to found his first monastery for those who wished to imitate his way of life, yet solitude was still his delight: 'Whoever lives in solitude has escaped three temptations: hearing, speaking and seeing, but against his own heart he must constantly battle.'

He set his brethren the example of prayer, humility and bodily mortification. He slept on the floor, ate hardly at all and underneath his tunic he wore a hair shirt. He exhorted them to care not for their bodies, to have eternity forever in their thoughts, to reflect every morning that they may not see the night and every evening that they may not see the sunrise. He encouraged them to resist the devil with vigour, to arm themselves with the sign of the cross. He told them how the devil had once appeared to him in glory and said: 'Ask what you will, I am the power of God.' He had invoked the name of Jesus and the devil vanished.

In 311 the Emperor Maximinus renewed his persecution of the Christians. Antony, hoping for the crown of martyrdom went to Alexandria to help and encourage the Christians condemned in the mines and dungeons, in the courts, at places of execution; blatantly wearing his white monastic habit, although he was never challenged. He returned to his monastery in 312 when the persecution died down, unharmed and, no doubt, bitterly disappointed.

Antony built another monastery, at Pispir on the banks of the River Nile, but he himself preferred to live in his remote cell on his mountain and it was there he had a vision. He saw the whole world covered so thickly in traps that it seemed impossible to tread without being caught in them. In alarm he cried out: 'Lord, who can escape them all?' A voice replied: 'Humility, O Antony!'

Antony engaged himself in a variety of manual tasks. After rising at midnight he watched most of the night, praying on his knees, hands uplifted till sunrise and sometimes into the afternoon. Those who visited him afflicted or distressed returned home full of comfort and joy. Many miraculous cures were wrought through him and he was granted heavenly visions and revelations.

Belacius, a general of Egypt was persecuting the Christians with zeal and fury. Antony wrote to him, asking that they may be left in peace. Belacius was furious. He ripped up the letter then he spat and trampled on it and threatened that Antony would be his victim. One day he was out riding with Nestorius, the governor of Egypt when his horse threw him. Then it bit him on the thigh and savaged him so severely that he died in agony three days later.

Antony made his last visitation of all his monks and foretold his own death. They begged that he should die among them but he chose to die where he had always lived, in his remote cell. He ordered that his body be buried in a secret place on his mountain, adding: 'On the day of the resurrection, I shall receive it incorruptible from the hand of God.' He embraced his disciples, calmly stretched out on the ground and breathed his last.

Antony died in the year 356. He was a hundred and five years old.

St Veronica, Abbess and Mystic

(1660-1727)
July 9

At the age of seventeen Ursula Giuliani was accepted as a novice at the Convent of the Poor Clares in Citta di Castello. Her devotion to the Passion of our Lord Jesus Christ inspired her to make Veronica her chosen name in religion, in honour of the holy woman who had made her way through the mob and the soldiers to wipe away the blood and sweat from the face of Our Saviour. (Tradition tells us that the impression of His divine countenance was left upon the cloth.)

Ursula was born at Mercatillo in the Duchy of Urbino, Italy, in 1660, the daughter of Francesco and Benedetta Giuliani. She was a prodigious child; at the age of six months she spoke the name of the Blessed Trinity and took her first steps. Like most saints her love for the poor began in childhood, and not content just to feed the hungry and give drink to the thirsty she also gave away some of her clothing when necessary.

From the age of eleven, our Lord's Sacred Passion began to fascinate her and become central to her devotions, together with a devout love and regard for our Blessed Lady, Christ's holy mother. Unfortunately, Ursula was critical of those whose zeal failed to match her own, but this relapse into pride was cured through a vision at the age of sixteen in which she saw her heart represented as a piece of steel.

Her father moved up in the world; he was appointed Intendant of Finance at Piacenza and, like all Continental parents, he began to seek an eligible suitor for his daughter. But in her heart Ursula had already pledged herself to God and her refusal of marriage aroused great opposition in the family home. As a result she became very ill and her father, realising her sincere desire for a life in the cloister, eventually gave his consent and blessing.

Yet there was something about the young Sr Veronica which distinguished her from the rest of the community. At the conclusion of the ceremony for her reception, the Bishop remarked privately to the Abbess: 'I commend this new daughter to your special care, for she will one day be a great saint.'

The way of those who seek spiritual perfection is hard, but Sr Veronica joyfully embraced the severities of the Order – long fasts, vigils, silence and to all these she added mortifications of her own. She cheerfully accepted the trials which God was pleased to send to her, but the extreme life of holiness and mortification she practised was ascribed to worldly reasons, to spiritual pride and in consequence she was treated with additional severity by her Superiors. In 1678 she was professed and in her prayers to Our Lord she expressed a desire to suffer with him for the conversion of sinners. It is said that at this time she was favoured again, with a vision of Jesus carrying the cross and then to feel an acute pain in her heart. Signs of the stigmata appeared on her in 1694: the mark of the Crown of Thorns on her head which brought excruciating and permanent pain. The Bishop of the diocese ordered that she should have medical treatment for her condition but this proved to be completely ineffectual.

At this time Sr Veronica was carrying out the difficult duties as Mistress of the Novices, yet despite being classed as a 'mystic' she was extremely practical in guiding those placed in her care. So practical that when she became Abbess in 1716 she had a better system of water pipes laid in the Convent and the whole place enlarged and improved.

Towards the end of her life she contracted apoplexy and this proved to be fatal. She died on 9 July 1727, after a life of intense interior suffering and, amazingly, the form of a cross was found impressed upon her heart.

St Maximilian Kolbe

(1984-1941)

August 14

'Greater love than this no man has, that he should lay down his life for his friends.'

These words of Our Lord perfectly sum up the heroic life and death of St Maximilian Kolbe and surely they were meant to have been inscribed on his gravestone. But there was no conventional grave for him, so no gravestone or the blessing of a Christian burial.

He was born on 7 January 1894 at Zdunska Wola, near Lodz in Poland and baptised Raymond, the second son of Jules Kolbe and Maria Dabrowska; there were also four other boys, Francis, Joseph, Valentine and Anthony. It was a happy, devout and holy family yet Raymond was a mischievous child and there were times when his mother just didn't know how to cope with him. But eventually, after he had prayed before the family shrine to Our Lady, in the living room of the home, Raymond began to realise the anguish he was causing his mother.

Yet Raymond's contrition had gone much further than the family shrine; while he was praying before Our Lady's altar in the church at Pabianice, Our Lady appeared to him. In her hands she carried two crowns: one red symbolising martyrdom, the other white for purity. She asked Raymond if he would like to choose a crown. 'I will choose both,' he replied. Our Lady smiled, then vanished from his sight.

It was a courageous choice for a ten-year-old boy and truly prophetic.

From then on Raymond devoted himself to good works, particularly in helping his mother – she certainly needed it. She had lost her two youngest sons, Valentine at the age of three and Anthony when he was just one year old, and she still worried about Raymond. Luckily the family fortunes improved, and the Kolbes moved into a small general store with Raymond and the other boys. Assisting in the store had no detrimental effect on Raymond's school work; academically he was brilliant, with a special talent for Latin. Fr Jankowski the parish priest noticed this and wondered what, exactly, the future held for the young and talented Raymond Kolbe.

It was in 1905 when Raymond and his brother Francis attended a retreat given by Fr Peregrine Haczela, the Franciscan Provincial. A few weeks later the boys heard that he was seeking candidates for the Franciscan secondary school at Lwow. They both applied and were accepted; Jules and Maria gave their blessing, even though they would miss their help in the store. They still had Joseph, but it proved to be only for a short time since he decided to follow in the footsteps of his brothers.

In 1907 Raymond and Francis joined the Franciscan Friary at Lwow. Here, Raymond excelled in mathematics and physics yet he had a passion for all things military and seriously considered a career in the army. Suddenly, his mother announced that as her three sons were now all in seminaries, she and Jules were going to enter into the religious life. So rather than upset his mother, Raymond abandoned his plans for a military career and instead joined the Franciscans as a novice in September 1910. He took the name of Maximilian.

In November 1912, Maximilian arrived in Rome with six companion Brothers; he was eighteen, and for the next three years they studied philosophy at the Gregorian College. Then from 1915 it was to be theology at the Collegio Serafico.

Yet throughout his long years of study an idea had formed then germinated in the mind of Maximilian, the notion of a spiritual weapon to fight the enemies of God. Then, on 17 October 1917, in a blinding flash of spiritual inspiration for the whole Christian world, Our Lady appeared at Fatima, in Portugal. And on that day Maximilian and six of his companions dedicated themselves as Crusaders, to strive for the conversion of sinners, to combat heretics, schismatics and the Freemasons. They consecrated themselves to Mary Immaculate and always wore the Miraculous Medal.

Maximilian was ordained priest on 28 April 1918 in the church of St Andrew della valle in Rome. He celebrated his first mass on the following day at the altar of the Virgin of Miracles in the church of St Andrew of Frate. The following year he completed his studies in theology but his health had become a problem: he was in an advanced state of TB.

Fr Maximilian returned to his native Poland in 1919 after the Great War was over and his return was extremely joyful, his country once more a free nation. Pope Pius XI had promulgated the Feast of Our Lady of Poland and Fr Maximilian declared his intention of winning every heart for Our Lady. In his crusade from his small monastery in Grodno he set up groups all over Poland even though doctors had pronounced his TB to be incurable. After a bout of pneumonia one lung was damaged, the other had collapsed and the doctors could do no more.

Yet Fr Maximilian continued to drive himself relentlessly in the pursuit of lost souls and soon he had turned to the written word. His first publication, a monthly journal called 'Knight of the Immaculate' began in 1922 with 5,000 copies printed, but it left him with a big problem: how was he going to pay the printer?

He travelled to Cracow and there in the Basilica of St Francis he prayed before the altar dedicated to Our Lady of the Seven Dolours. When he had finished telling Our Lady of his financial plight he suddenly noticed an envelope lying on the altar. It was addressed: 'To you, O Mother Immaculate'. He opened it and inside was the exact amount of money required to pay the printer.

The situation improved, more funds became available and in 1927 the circulation of the 'Knight' had risen to an astonishing 70,000. But Grodno monastery could no longer sustain such a mammoth operation, so in November 1927 the Franciscans moved to Teresin. In December the monastery was consecrated and given the name 'Niepokalaow' – the City of the Immaculate. In the beginning it consisted of just a few old shacks with tar paper roofs, earthen floors and crude furniture, yet soon vocations poured in from all over Poland. Later, in 1939, it was to become probably the largest friary in the world with 762 inhabitants, 13 priests, 18 novices, 527 brothers, 122 boys in the junior seminary, and 82 candidates for the priesthood. Totally self-supporting with doctors, dentists, farmers, builders...

Demand for the 'Knight' continued to grow, reaching a staggering 750,000 copies a month. A Catholic newspaper followed in 1935 with 137,000 daily copies and 220,000 on Sundays and Holy Days. There were also a number of companion publications, each with impressive circulations. In 1938 a radio station was installed to spread ever further the word of God and 'Niepokalaow' could by now boast of its own fire brigade.

But in 1930 the thoughts of Fr Maximilian had turned to work in the missionary fields, in Japan. But why Japan? Was he seeking his crown of red (remembering the Japanese Martyrs) or was it an incident on the train journey from Zakopane to Grodno he recalled when he met a party of Japanese travellers. He was heart broken to discover they had never heard of the Blessed Virgin Mary and he gave each of them a Miraculous Medal. On 26 February of that year he left Poland with four brothers for the Far East, with calls at Lourdes and Lisieux along the way. On 24 April 1930 they arrived at Nagasaki (two of the brothers had disembarked for work in Shanghai) to be greeted by Archbishop Hayaska. When he discovered that Fr Maximilian had two doctorates they did a deal of mutual assistance: Fr Maximilian would take the vacant chair of philosophy in the diocesan seminary and the Archbishop would give his blessing to the publication and distribution of the 'Knight'.

It was hard going for Fr Maximilian and his companions. Wretched accommodation, little knowledge of the native language and meagre resources, yet incredibly a month later the first Japanese 'Knight' was in circulation. A year later the first Japanese 'Niepokalaow' was operational, built on the slopes of Mount Hikosan. The site was cheap and far from ideal yet its location was later to prove fortuitous. When the atomic bomb was dropped on Nagasaki in 1945, the mountain protected it from the full force of the blast and the inhabitants survived. Today it is the fulcrum of the Franciscan province.

In his constant crusade in the pursuit of souls Fr Maximilian proved to be a wise missionary. He did not attempt to force Western ideals on the native population and he built up a good working relationship with the leaders of other religions. The Japanese 'Knight' was an instant success and by 1936 the circulation had steadily risen to a commendable 65,000. Offers of help poured in and the number of vocations was growing but he was still in extremely poor health. There were times when he had to be supported during mass and on one occasion one of the brothers found him lying in the road where he had collapsed from exhaustion.

Yet his zeal remained unquenched, as did his thirst for knowledge. He travelled through Siberia and spent some time in Moscow where he studied the insidious ideals of Marxism. In 1936 he was recalled to Poland. He had hoped to find martyrdom in Japan (how wistfully he had gazed up at the Mount of the Martyrs) and in a way he had – he had endured constant ill-health, violent headaches, a rich variety of trials and tribulations and he was covered in abscesses.

Suddenly World War II exploded; Poland was invaded and 'Niepokalaow' was occupied by German forces with most of the inhabitants deported to Germany, as was Fr Maximilian. Then, inexplicably they were released and Fr Maximilian returned to 'Niepokalaow', to organise relief for 3,000 refugees (including 2,000 Jews). Still the 'Knight' was printed, but a provocative article by Fr Maximilian enraged the Nazis and he was arrested. It was February 1941 and he was taken to the infamous Pawiak prison in Warsaw. Here he was ridiculed and beaten for wearing his Franciscan habit, his symbol of Christianity, then it was confiscated and he was given a prison uniform.

In the following May Fr Maximilian was transferred to Auschwitz along with three hundred other prisoners, this time with a striped prison uniform and a number: 16670. Despite his obvious ill-health he was put to work carrying blocks of stone, then later he was sent with other priests to the Babice section under the command of 'Bloody Krott', an ex-criminal. The Commandant condemned the priests as layabouts and parasites and ordered Krott to 'get them working!'

Krott did, the priests heaving and carrying huge tree trunks in fair weather or foul, all day without a break and at the double. Krott had developed an insidious dislike of Fr Maximilian, so he gave him the heavier tasks and, despite having only one lung he could not escape the vicious beatings from the guards when he flagged. His friends would try to help, but he refused rather than expose them to further punishment. Krott's hatred for the holy man continued to grow; on one occasion he personally piled heavy planks of wood on the Franciscan's back, then ordered him to run until he eventually collapsed into the mud. Krott kicked him in the stomach, the guards gave him fifty lashes and left him for dead. His companions rescued him and managed to get him to the *Revier*, the camp hospital.

The ill-treatment Fr Maximilian received did not affect the fire of his love for his fellow men. Secretly, he heard confessions, took last place in the queue for the meagre food ration and if he did get any he very often shared it, or gave it away. His fellow prisoners gathered in secret to hear his words of love and encouragement – a living saint in the guise of an impoverished beggar, a tin can hanging from his belt.

One dark day in July 1941 the camp siren sounded to signify there had been an escape. The inmates were lined up in the street between Blocks 14 and 17, a count was taken and it was discovered that three prisoners were missing. Lagerfuhrer Fritzsch announced that as a reprisal ten of the inmates would be confined to the Bunker (the underground starvation cell).

Franciszek Gajowniczek, one of the men selected broke down and cried out in despair, 'O my poor wife, my poor children. I shall never see them again.'

Out from the ragged ranks Fr Maximilian stepped forward and stood to attention. A vision from his childhood, the red crown was drawing near. Then he spoke to the German officer. Fritzsch listened, nodded, pointed and Fr Maximilian took the place of Gajowniczek in the death group. A command was given and they were all marched off to Block 13, the death block, the airless underground cells to be stripped and where they would slowly die without food or water.

Already there were twenty dying men in there for all of them death was close at hand but the Faith was alive and at least they had a priest with them to help them die. Fervent prayers and hymns to Our Lady transformed the dreaded death bunker into a cathedral and Fr Maximilian was their pastor. The SS responded with vicious beatings to subdue the pathetic congregation, devotions turned to anguished cries for food and water and the cries became desperate and ever more persistent. Fr Maximilian did not beg or complain, but remained standing or kneeling among the prostate bodies and the whispered prayers to cheerfully face the brutal SS. Yet even they grudgingly acknowledged his bravery: 'Never have we seen anything like it. Never such a man as this.'

One by one they died, each of them comforted by the Franciscan till he alone was left, the only living thing in a pile of emaciated corpses. Two weeks had passed since they had entered the death chamber and the Camp authorities considered this to be long enough; the cells were required for new victims. The head of sick quarters, a criminal named Bock was ordered to administer a lethal injection to the sole survivor. The needle pierced the scrawny left arm with carbolic acid, and this saint of the Bunker slumped down to the floor, eyes wide open, his face calm and radiant. It was 14 August 1941 and he was forty-seven years old.

There was no Christian burial. His body was placed in a crude wooden coffin (a privilege begged by his friends) then thrown into the camp incinerator. His ashes scattered in the wind, to sanctify wherever they fell; love had conquered hatred and Fr Maximilian

Kolbe, the small boy who had devoted his life to Mary Immaculate had received his red crown of martyrdom.

On 10 October 1982 he was canonised. The earthly misery and degradation of the concentration camps had been transformed into eternal glory.

Blessed Karl Leisner
(1915-1945)

The Nazi concentration camps of the World War II era
housed many saints, most of them known only to God
himself. But there are some whose heroic lives and
deaths *are* known to us, their names an everlasting
testament to those who lived and died in the noble
cause of humanity in opposing a cruel and evil regime.
Many victims died for the Faith, a faith which would
not and could not compromise despite threats, brutality
and torture; a tragic example of man's inhumanity to
man which began with the rise to power of Adolf Hitler
in the years following World War I.

The self-elevation of Hitler to Chancellor proved to
be a disaster waiting to happen. Germany had emerged
from the war humiliated, impoverished and leaderless.
Kaiser Wilhelm II had fled to Holland and the Weimar
Republic was set up, eventually collapsing in a wave
of disastrous unemployment, galloping inflation and
bread queues. So it was relatively easy for a determined
character like Hitler to achieve ultimate power by stealth
and skulduggery. His enemies eliminated, Hitler was
now *der Führer* (the Leader) and only one stumbling
block remained in his path, the Catholic Church.
Eventually it would be dealt with, but for the time
being life would be made very uncomfortable.

It was in the menacing year of 1934, a year after
Hitler had come to power, that Karl Leisner decided
that he wanted to become a priest. He was born on

28 February 1915, at Rees-am-Rhein. When he was six the family moved to Cleves, a city on the Lower Rhine remembered for its strong connections with Anne of Cleves, one of the failed wives of Henry VIII. Much of his early life was devoted to working among the youth of Cleves, a task becoming increasingly difficult in the face of the belligerent Nazi Youth.

Karl was admitted as a student for the priesthood at the Collegium Borromeum by Bishop von Galem of Munster, an uncompromising opponent of Nazism who appointed him Diocesan Youth Leader. This post had become too dangerous for a layman because those who worked for the Church became marked men, but Karl could operate from the relative safety of the seminary. He regarded his task as an honour, yet it also was dangerous as he had to travel around the diocese by train and bicycle in the face of constant intimidation.

There were two hundred and eighty students at the seminary and life was austere. The day started with prayer in the chapel at 5.30 a.m. then Mass, breakfast – a cup of coffee at 7 a.m. with the first lecture at 7.15 a.m. Then more lectures, periods of silence, physical exercise, breaks for lunch and dinner, prayer and lights out at 10 p.m.

After studying philosophy at Munster for two years, Karl transferred to the University of Freiburg for a course in Dogmatic and Moral Theology. He lodged with a local family, only to find himself falling in love with Elisabeth, the daughter of his host; he had never experienced anything like it. Day after day, week after week, Karl agonised over the problem: should he choose the vocation of marriage or vocation to the priesthood? Complete dedication was essential whichever path he chose.

Karl left Freiburg in March 1935 and he had made his decision. He wrote to Elisabeth telling her that he must be a priest. Karl had chosen the spiritual path – it would be a hard and rocky road.

The next six months found Karl doing National Service on the land; there he had to cope with Nazi propaganda and the vilification of the Catholic Church, yet he had a good influence on the other conscripts and even organised Sunday Mass attendance. It didn't go unnoticed; the Nazi authorities marked him as dangerous and on 29 October 1937 his home in Cleves was raided by the Gestapo, searched and all his private papers confiscated.

Karl continued his studies for the priesthood and despite an attack of pleurisy he was ordained deacon in Munster Cathedral by Bishop von Galen on 25 March 1939. His joy was overwhelming, then tragedy: by the end of the year he had tuberculosis in both lungs. In those days, TB as it was known, was equivalent to a death sentence, yet with care and good food and his own natural strength, Karl made a good recovery at the Sankt Blasien sanatorium.

On 8 November 1939 a time-bomb left in a hall in Munich exploded. Hitler had just left, so the attempt on his life had failed but Karl was heard to remark that it was a pity he wasn't in the hall. A police van arrived at the sanatorium and he was arrested by the Gestapo. As he was taken away, the young man who had betrayed him came up grief-stricken to apologise in tears. Karl said, 'Do not cry for me. I forgive you.'

He spent the following winter in Freiburg gaol as a political prisoner and on 16 March 1940 he was transferred to Sachsenhausen concentration camp. On 14 December he was taken to Dachau where he was stripped naked, head-shaved and dressed in striped jacket and trousers, a cap and wooden clogs. The inmates were deprived of all human dignity, even a name – Karl Leisner became No. 22356. The food was mainly a meagre diet of ersatz coffee and black bread, a little soup and coarse sausage.

The SS guards attempted to break their spirit with frequent beatings and the threat of pathological sadism in the punishment block, and the tall chimney of the crematorium smoked unceasingly as the bodies of those who had died were disposed of. Executions were frequent, as were the suicides of the inmates who flung themselves onto the electrified fence surrounding the camp. During the typhoid epidemics, the crematorium couldn't cope so communal graves had to be dug.

Dachau had been built to accommodate 6,000 prisoners but at the end there were 33,000, so at the age of twenty-five Karl found himself in an over-crowded hell on earth, yet he remained cheerful, tried to keep himself fit and he would often give his bread ration away to others. The winter of 1941 was extremely severe, the spring soaking wet; the prisoners spent day and night in wet clothes and Karl's TB came back. Then one night, during a routine inspection, two SS guards beat Karl so badly that he was taken to the camp hospital, spitting blood and housed in a room crowded with delirious and at times violent patients. Yet as the disease ate into his lungs he acted to appear fitter than he was as the incurable were sent to the gas chambers at Schloss Hartheim.

There were times when Karl was close to despair, and amidst all the suffering it seemed that God did not hear his prayers. Then in September 1944, a surprise: Bishop Piguet, a Frenchman arrived. He had been arrested for helping people to escape from the Germans by issuing false documents. Someone suggested that he could ordain Karl in the camp; the Bishop agreed and Karl was delighted but there were difficulties to surmount. They had to get permission from Bishop von Galen, and they needed chrism for the anointing and a Pontifical, the book containing the text of the rite.

Amazingly, all these items were obtained through the underground network set up by prisoners working in the camp garden. So Karl Leisner was ordained priest on 17 December 1944 in a moving and unique ceremony in the midst of squalor and suffering. A fellow prisoner painted his ordination card showing two hands in chains holding a chalice with the inscription *Sacerdotem oportet offere:* 'a priest must offer up'. For most of the Mass Karl was so weak that he sat slumped on a *prie-dieu,* and was so exhausted at the end that he went straight back to the hospital.

It was not until 26 December that Karl was well enough to celebrate his first Mass. He had always dreamed that it would be in his home town of Cleves, but he knew it had been flattened by Allied bombs. Now his only home was Dachau and here he celebrated. Somehow his fellow prisoners had begged or borrowed cups, coffee and cake and there were flowers on the makeshift altar. So Fr Karl Leisner said his first Mass and it was also to be his last; he was too ill ever to say Mass again.

On 29 April 1945 American tanks arrived at Dachau, the SS surrendered but after five and a half years in captivity it was all too late for Fr Karl. On 4 May he was taken away from the heaps of corpses, the living skeletons and the hideous stench to a sanatorium at Planegg, near Munich. He received the Last Sacraments from his friend, Fr Otto Pies, then a few weeks later, on 29 June, quite incredibly, his father and mother arrived having made their way through all the military zones and devastation to visit their son. His mother was with him when he died on 12 August 1945 with a prayer for his friends... and for his enemies.

The story of Karl Leisner is a reflection of all those who suffered and perished in the Nazi concentration camps. The story of a priest who said just one Mass in his life on this earth, like Jesus at the Last Supper.

He was beatified by Pope John Paul II on 23 June 1996, ironically in the Olympic Stadium, Berlin, built by Adolf Hitler.

St Sebastian

(3rd century)

January 20

It would appear that Sebastian was a brave Christian double agent at the time of the violent persecutions of the Emperor Diocletian. A native of Norbonne in France, he was brought up in Milan and from there he went to Rome where he joined the army about the year 283. This was not because he wanted to be a soldier, but to be better able, and without suspicion to assist the Christians who were under constant persecution.

Marcus and Marcellianus were Christians under the sentence of death; their faith was being shaken by the pleas of family and friends to submit and save their own lives. Sebastian encouraged them with a fiery eloquence which produced extraordinary results. Zoe, the wife of Nicostratus the Master of the Rolls, who had been dumb for six years fell at the feet of Sebastian and spoke quite distinctly when he made the sign of the cross on her tongue. Her husband was converted to the Faith, as were the parents of Marcus and Marcellianus together with Claudius the jailer and sixteen other prisoners. Nicostratus, who was in charge of the prisoners took them all to his own house where the holy priest Polycarp baptised them.

Chromatius, the Governor of Rome was informed; he was also told that Tranquillus, the father of Marcus and Marcellianus had been cured of gout on being baptised. On hearing this he decided to be instructed in the Faith, as he himself suffered from the same illness. He sent for Sebastion who cured him, then he was baptised together with his son Tiburtius. He released all the prisoners in his charge, set his slaves free and resigned his position. Chromatius then retired to the countryside of Campania and took many of the new converts with him.

There was now a decision to be made: would it be Polycarp or Sebastian who would go with them? The answer came from Pope Caius – Polycarp went and Sebastian stayed as a soldier in the city to help and encourage the Christians, a difficult task which became decidedly dangerous in 286 when the persecution intensified.

The heat was on so much that Pope Caius had to take refuge, right inside the Imperial Palace in the rooms of Castulus, a Christian officer of the Court. Zoe was the first to be arrested while she was praying at the tomb of St Peter; she was martyred by smoke, hanging head down over a fire. When Tranquillus went to pray at the tomb of St Paul he was seized by the crowd and stoned to death. Nicostratus, Claudius, Castorius and Victorinus were all captured, tortured three times and then thrown into the sea. Tiburtius was betrayed by a friend and beheaded. Castulus was also betrayed by the same false friend, racked three times then buried alive. Marcellianus was nailed to a post, left in agony for a day and a night then shot to death by arrows.

Sebastion, having watched so many of his friends tortured and martyred was now impeached and brought before the dreaded Emperor Diocletian. He fiercely reproached Sebastian for his ingratitude and ordered him to be killed by arrows. The sentence was carried out and he was left for dead, his body shot and pierced, but when Irene, the widow of St Castulus was about to bury him, she found him still alive. She managed to get him back to her house, where she nursed him back to health.

Yet Sebastian refused to flee the persecution; in fact, he did quite the opposite. He waylaid the Emperor to reproach him for his cruel persecution of the Christians. The Emperor was astonished – Sebastian was supposed to be dead. He recovered from this amazing confrontation and ordered Sebastian to be clubbed to death and his body thrown into a sewer.

After his death, the martyr, in effect a double martyr, appeared in a vision to a pious lady named Lucina. She found his body; it was pulled out of the sewer and honourably interred in the catacombs in the cemetery of Calistus, at the place where the church of San Sebastian now stands.

St Francis of Assisi
(1182-1226)
October 4

Despite the fact that St Francis died way back in the year 1226 it seems he is still universally loved and admired almost as if he were still alive today. His spirit lives on.

He was born at Assisi in Italy in 1182, the son of Peter and Pica Bernardon and baptised John. But as his wealthy parents did much business in France and because the boy was so proficient in the language, he became known as Francis. As a young man he liked to enjoy himself yet he was always kind to the poor, meek and patient. That virtue was tested to the full when, in the local war between Perugia and Assisi he was, with several others, captured and imprisoned for a year. As a result of this experience he suffered a long and dangerous sickness. After his recovery he rode out one day in a new suit of clothes and on the road he met a gentleman reduced to poverty and poorly clad. Francis felt so sorry for the gentleman that he exchanged clothes with him.

That night, in a dream, he saw a magnificent palace filled with arms marked with the sign of the cross. A voice told him that they were for his soldiers if they would take up the cross and fight under its banner. An inner strength awakened in him and with it the desire to attain perfect mortification of himself and his senses. Out riding again on the plains of Assisi he met a leper. He recoiled with horror at the sight of his sores, but overcame that horror and as the leper stretched out his hand to receive alms, Francis kissed it.

He now resolved to aim at Christian perfection. He begged our Lord to reveal to him his will and at a time of meditation, totally absorbed in God, he seemed to see a vision of Christ hanging on the cross. From that time he was fired with acts of poverty, love and piety – to visit hospitals and serve the sick, to serve them all as if he were serving Christ himself.

Francis journeyed to Rome to visit the tombs of the Apostles and finding a crowd of poor people at the door of St Peter's church, he gave his clothes to the poorest among them in exchange for the man's rags, just as he had done at home in Assisi. His pilgrimage over, he was one day praying in the Church of St Damian before a crucifix when he seemed to hear a voice coming from it to say, three times in all: 'Francis, repair my house which you see is falling'.

He went home, found a load of cloth in his father's warehouse and took it by horse to Foligni where he sold it – and the horse. He took the money to the poor old priest at St Damians and asked if he could stay with him. The priest agreed that he could but would not accept the money, so Francis left it on a window sill. His father soon found out what he had done and raged into St Damians, but he was quickly pacified when he discovered the money on the window sill. Francis in the meantime had hid himself, then after days of fasting and prayer he emerged on to the streets of Assisi, but because he looked like a beggar he was pelted and abused and called a madman, all of which he bore with great joy.

His father wasn't pleased. He dragged Francis home, beat him unmercifully, put fetters on his feet then locked him in a room but his mother released him when his father went out. Francis returned to St Damians but his father followed him, insisting that he should either return home or renounce his inheritance before the bishop. Francis did renounce his inheritance, before the Bishop of Assisi. He took off his clothes and gave them to his father and by this gesture he renounced the world. The bishop admired his humility and fervour, and the cloak of a servant was brought for him. Francis chalked a cross on the cloak then he put it on. This happened in 1206, when he was twenty-five.

Francis went out from the bishop's palace to walk to the city of Gubbio, where a friend furnished him with clothes. In the hospital there he cared for the lepers and gathered alms for the repair of the church of St Damians; he then carried the stones and laboured to help the stonemasons, eventually leaving the church in a good state of repair.

He now went to a little church called Portiuncula belonging to the Benedictine monks of Subiaco and situated about a mile from Assisi.

The church was dedicated, much to the delight of Francis, to Our Lady of Angels and almost falling down. In 1207 he set to work to repair it, made his home close by, and made the church the heart of his devotions. Here he spent two years, then hearing one day the words of Christ in the Gospel, 'Do not carry gold or silver or food for your journey nor two coats or a staff,' Francis gave all his money and his belongings, leaving himelf only an old coat tied at the waist with a rope.

This was to be the habit he gave to his friends the following year.

About this time a man from Spoletto came to see him, suffering from a running cancer which had corrupted his mouth and cheeks hideously. He had tried all remedies, even making several pilgrimages to Rome; Francis was his last desperate hope. Francis kissed his ulcerous sore which was instantly healed.

The agony of Christ on the cross was at the heart of all his devotions: 'I weep for the sufferings of my Lord Jesus Christ...' Many began to admire this great servant of God and some desired to be his companion. The first was Bernard, a rich man of Assisi who invited him to stay at his house. He watched Francis secretly at night and saw him spend the whole time praying on his knees while repeating: '*Deus meus et omnia*': 'My God and my all'.

Bernard was convinced of the sanctity of Francis and begged him to make him his companion. They prayed and heard Mass together to discover the will of God: Bernard sold everything, and gave the money to the poor. Peter of Catana, a canon of the cathedral of Assisi had the same intentions as Bernard; Francis gave the habit to both of them on 16 August 1209, which is regarded as the official date of the founding of the Order. The third person to join was Giles, a simple man of great virtue. The Order was granted verbal approval by the Pope in the same year.

Francis returned from Rome with his little band of followers to settle in an old abandoned cottage at Rivo-Torto near Assisi. Soon they moved to Portiuncula; the number of followers had risen to one hundred and twenty-five and Francis gave them a Rule for his Order consisting of the gospel counsels of perfection, manual labour and not being ashamed to beg, remembering the poverty of Christ. He took his Rule to Rome, eventually receiving verbal approval from the Pope, who in a vision had seen Francis supporting the Lateran church. The Pope also ordained him deacon. (The Order was officially confirmed by Pope Honorius III on 29 November 1223.)

Francis and his followers decided to reside in the cottage at Rivo-Torto where they lived in a spirit of holy poverty. 'Poverty is the way to salvation, the cradle of humility and the root of perfection.' Soon after, the Benedictines of Monte Soubazo gave them the use of the church at Portiuncula.

Holy poverty was dear to the heart of Francis, as was his extraordinary love of penance. His bed was the ground and he slept propped up on a piece of wood or a stone. He ate little and then only coarse bread, drank only water, fasted rigorously eight 'Lents' a year and to his extreme austerities he added humility of heart. So great was his humility that he would not be ordained priest and he remained a deacon.

His desire for the conversion of souls was ardent, so intense that he resolved to go and preach to the Muhammadans and other infidels. In the sixth year after his conversion he embarked for Syria but a tempest drove the vessel on to the coast of Dalmatia; unable to progress any further, Francis had to return to Ancona. The next year, in 1214, he set out for Morocco to preach to the exalted Muhammadan King Miramolin. But in Spain he was taken ill, suffered various accidents and was delayed by the business of his Order so he could not possibly continue. Nevertheless, he worked several miracles in Spain, founded new houses and returned to Languedoc in Italy.

Francis preached penance to the world, often saying, 'My love is crucified', meaning that Christ is crucified so we also should crucify our flesh. He gave his Order the name of the Friars Minor and founded convents at Cortona, Arezzo, Vergoreta, Pisa, Bologna, Florence and in many other places. In less than three years there were sixty monasteries.

In 1212 Francis gave the habit to Clare, (later to become a saint) and she, under his direction founded the Second Order of St Francis, for women. When St Dominic visited Rome in 1215 he met Francis there and together they had frequent conferences to cement the friendship of their Orders.

In 1219 Francis held the famous General Chapter near Portiuncula. Five thousand friars met there but others were obviously not able to leave their monasteries. In the same year, Francis set out with his companions to sail to Palestine and there he met up with the Christian army of the Sixth Crusade. Francis, foretelling the defeat of the Christians against overwhelming Saracen odds tried to persuade them not to attack. The army commanders didn't listen, the Christians were driven back and six thousand men were lost, but later they were to be victorious.

Francis, burning with zeal to convert the Saracens, made his way towards their camp only to be captured by a guard. 'I am a Christian,' Francis told him, 'take me to your master.'

Taken before the Sultan he said, 'I am sent not by men but by the most high God to show you and your people the way to salvation, by proclaiming to you the truth of the Gospel.'

The Sultan was much impressed by his fervour and eloquence and invited him to stay.

Francis replied, 'If you and your people will hear the word of God I will gladly stay with you. But if you cannot decide between Christ and Muhammad, let a great fire be lit and I will go into it with your Imams that you may see which is the true faith.'

The Sultan refused, believing that none of the priests would go into the fire with Francis, but he did offer many presents which Francis refused. After some days the Sultan, fearful that some of his men should be converted by his preaching and desert to the enemy, sent him under escort back to the Christian camp, but quietly saying before Francis left, 'Pray for me, that God will make known to me the one true religion and guide me to it.'

Francis returned to Italy, only to hear that the five missionaries he had sent to the Moors had all received the crown of martyrdom. He resigned the generalship of the Order in 1220 with the virtuous Peter of Catana taking his place. In 1215, Count Orlando had built a convent for the friars on Mount Alverno. Its peace and solitude were a joy to Francis, as were the raptures and the extraordinary favours he received from God, and there were times when he was raised up from the ground while in prayer. The year 1224 saw Francis living in a little secret cell on the mountainside. He kept Brother Leo, his confessor with him and in this lonely place, heavenly visions and communications with the Holy Spirit were familiar to him.

It was here that he saw an angel with six shining wings blazing with fire and bearing down on him from heaven. Within the wings there appeared the figure of a man crucified. Francis beheld the sight with amazement and joy, yet the sorrowful sight pierced his soul with a sword of compassion; the vision disappeared and Francis was left with the seal of Christ's crucifixion: the marks of black nails in his hands and feet, right through as if hammered, his side pierced as if lanced. Francis did his best to conceal the stigmata, wearing socks and boots on his feet and covering his hands, yet these miraculous wounds were seen by others during the two years until his death. After his death many were to witness this divine favour in recognition of the love of Francis for Christ on the cross.

During that last two years of his life there was more to suffer in sickness and weakness, and pains in his eyes. In his violent pain he prayed, 'O Lord, I give thee thanks for the pain I suffer.' He foretold his own death and when the time came he insisted that he be laid on the ground and covered with an old habit. He exhorted his brethren to love God, poverty and patience, then he gave his last blessing: 'Farewell my children, remain always in the fear of the Lord... I hasten to go to him, to whose grace I recommend you all.'

The Passion of Our Lord Jesus Christ was read and Francis yielded up his soul to God on 4 October 1226. He was forty-five years old.

Prayer of St Francis

Lord, make me an instrument of your peace.
Where there is hatred, let me sow love.
Where there is injury, let me sow pardon.
Where there is friction, let me sow union.
Where there is error, let me sow truth.
Where there is doubt, let me sow faith.
Where there is despair, let me sow hope.
Where there is darkness, let me sow light.
Where there is sadness, let me sow joy.
O Divine Master,
grant that I may not so much seek
to be consoled as to console,
to be understood as to understand,
to be loved as to love.
For it is in giving that we receive.
It is in pardoning that we are pardoned.
It is in dying that we are born to eternal life.
Amen.

St Francis will ever be remembered for the good things he did and the great things which happened to him. For his preaching to the birds and his love of animals, for giving us the first Christmas crib and in it the little child who woke up when St Francis took him in his arms.

St Winifred
(7th century)
November 3

According to venerable historians, Winifred, or Wenefrede as she was originally known, lived in the 7th century, the beautiful daughter of Thevith, a rich nobleman in the Kingdom of North Wales. Her virtuous parents desired that she should be instructed in the Christian Faith and when St Beuno, her mother's uncle settled in the district, Winifred was happy to take the religious veil and with other holy women consecrated her virginity to God.

Her father gave St Beuno land to build a church and later a convent for the holy women, and St Beuno was their spiritual director. After the death of St Beuno, Winifred left, eventually joining a convent in Denbighshire under the direction of the holy abbot Elerius. When Theonia the abbess died, Winifred was chosen as her successor.

Yet Caradoc, the son of the noble prince Alain had violently fallen in love with her. So great was his passion, then rage at her rejection that one day when she was fleeing from his unwanted attentions, he cut off her head at the place now known as Holywell,

Robert of Shrewsbury and others maintain that the earth opened and swallowed Caradoc up. Where the head of Winifred fell, the well which can be seen there today sprang up, the stones in the crystal clear water stained with red streaks. It is also believed that Winifred was brought back to life by the prayers of St Beuno and she bore thereafter a red circle around her neck, the sign of her martyrdom.

Her relics were taken to Shrewsbury in 1138, to the Benedictine Abbey built in 1083 by the Earl of Montgomery and plundered at the dissolution of the monasteries in the time of Henry VIII,

Many miraculous cures have been obtained at Shrewsbury and Holywell through the intercession of St Winifred.

Sir Roger Bodenham, Knight of the Bath was abandoned by the ablest physicians in the land, yet he was cured of leprosy in the year 1606 when he bathed in the water at Holywell.

A Mrs Jane Wakeman was cured in 1630 of an ulcerated breast when she bathed three times in the water.

A poor widow of Kidderminster was lame and bedridden. She sent a single penny to Holywell with instructions that it should be given to the first poor person to be met. At the exact time the penny was given, the poor widow of Kidderminster was cured. This fact was attested by Mr James Bridges, who was later to become the sheriff of Worcester in 1651.

A Mrs Mary Newman had been reduced to a skeleton by eighteen years of illness and was hardly able to walk. The best physicians in Europe had all tried and failed, yet she was cured when she bathed for the fifth time in the waters of Holywell.

Many other cures are recorded, a living testimony to the sanctity of St Winifred, the holy virgin.

St Edward the Confessor
(AD 1066)
October 13

It is probably true to say that kings of a former age wielded ultimate power and ruled through fear and patronage. Few were rewarded with loyalty by ruling with love and kindness, but Edward the Confessor was an exception to the rule.

He was the son of King Ethelred II and educated in the palace of the Duke of Normandy, and from his infancy it was his delight to pray, to attend Holy Mass and visit churches and monasteries. His character was that of the exemplary Christian, marked with a spirit of humility and universal charity – ambition could find no place in his heart. He was crowned king on Easter day 1042, being about forty years of age.

He ascended to the throne at a most difficult time both at home and abroad. The Danes had been barbarously troublesome for the past forty years having colonised the kingdoms of Northumberland, Mercia and East Anglia, yet such was their respect for Edward they gave him no trouble. The only war Edward undertook was to restore Malcolm, King of Scotland and this ended in glorious victory.

Edward's virtuous life was a powerful example to those at court and to his advisers and friends. He refused to raise taxes and when the King's exchequer was exhausted by his alms-giving, the lords of the kingdom raised a large sum of money from the king's subjects to replenish it. Edward extended his thanks to his lords and ordered that every penny should be returned.

From his youth Edward greatly respected holy purity, a love sustained by humility, prayer and mortification, which he deployed against the violent assaults and cunning devices of the devil. Yet his nobles and people entreated him to take a royal consort, and Earl Godwin was delighted when Edward chose his daughter to be his wife. Edgitha was a beautiful and virtuous young lady, intelligent and understanding, and when Edward suggested (after much devout prayer) that they should live like the Blessed Virgin Mary and St Joseph in holy virginity, she readily agreed. After being joined in Holy Matrimony they lived ever after like brother and sister.

Despite the virtuous reign of the king enemies tried to bring him down and with him the whole administration. They conceived a cunning plot to attack him through the queen mother. Queen Emma frequently met with Alwin, the pious Bishop of Winchester who was her adviser on spiritual matters. She was accused of criminal conversation with him, of having agreed to marry Canute, the enemy of her former husband's family, of favouring Hardicanute and so endangering the whole Saxon dynasty. Robert, Archbishop of Canterbury was persuaded of her guilt, and the further accusation of sacrilege filled Edward with horror and grief.

He ordered an assembly of bishops at Winchester to consider the charges. Several of the bishops wished the charges to be dropped but the Archbishop of Canterbury was against this. Emma, having prayed to God in her distress placed her complete trust in Divine providence, offering herself to the trial of ordeal. Following a night spent in imploring Divine intercession, she walked blindfolded and barefoot over nine red hot ploughshares laid in the Church of St Swithin, remaining totally unscathed. The blindfold removed, she looked back disbelievingly at the red hot ploughshares then burst into praises of God for her miraculous deliverance. King Edward fell tearfully at her feet and begged forgiveness for his credulity, and in expiation was flogged by two bishops. Archbishop Robert retired to his monastery in Normandy after his penance of making a pilgrimage to Rome. Emma, the queen mother died at Winchester in 1052.

The years following were unique in their variety of deaths. Earl Godwin fell down dead while having supper with the king. It had been said that the king still suspected Godwin of arranging his brother Alfred's death. Godwin stated that if he were guilty of this he would never swallow the piece of meat he was putting into his mouth. He choked on it.

Harold succeeded his father Godwin in the earldom of Kent. Griffith, the Prince of South Wales invaded Herefordshire and the king ordered Harold to curb him. Griffith was later captured by the Prince of North Wales and put to death; his head was sent to Harold together with gifts for King Edward. In 1058 the king's great friend, the pious and valiant Earl Siward died and his death was followed by that of Leofric, another great friend and a model of Christian perfection. His wife, the charitable Lady Godiva is remembered as a praiseworthy patron of the city of Coventry.

The laws framed by King Edward were the result of

his wisdom and wise counselling and they still form the basis of the common law of England. Public peace and tranquillity were maintained, and property secured by the diligence with which the laws were executed.

King Edward made a vow to make a pilgrimage to St Peter's tomb in Rome. But after making all the necessary preparations his advisors declared that while commending his devotion, his absence would leave the kingdom exposed to the Danes, slaughter, domestic divisions and every other disaster.

The king was undecided, so he referred the matter to the Pope, Leo IX. After consideration, the Pope released him from his vow on condition that he gave the cost of his journey to the poor and built or repaired a monastery, to be endowed in honour of St Peter. He fulfilled the Pope's conditions at the monastery of St Peter, at a place now called Westminster. It was while Edward resided at his palace close by that he cured an Irishman named Gillemichel who was crippled and covered in running sores. He also cured a woman who came to him after being urged to do so in a dream. The king washed and blessed the ulcerous sore on her swollen chin and the sore burst and cleansed itself. It was reported that the king healed many others, and so began the legend of the king's touch.

King Edward decided on Christmas as the time for the dedication of the church at Westminster. He had a great devotion to St John the Evangelist who forewarned the king of his approaching death. Edward was taken ill before the dedication ceremony was over but he managed to stay to the conclusion. He breathed his last with his nobles bathed in tears round his deathbed, his affectionate wife weeping bitterly. 'Weep not,' he said to her, 'I shall die, but I shall live. Departing from the land of the dying, I hope to see the good things of the Lord in the land of the living.'

Commending her to the care of his brother Harold, he calmly expired on 5 January 1066 having reigned for twenty-three years. He was sixty-four.

In 1102 the body of St Edward was found to be incorrupt. Shortly after, a cripple was cured after praying at his tomb, and six blind men also recovered their sight.

Out of respect for the memory of St Edward, the monarchs of England to this day, at their coronation receive the crown of St Edward and put on his dalmatic and maniple as part of the royal robes.

He was canonised in 1161.

The Forty Martyrs of Sebaste

(AD 320)
March 10

These forty soldiers of the Thundering Legion, so famous under Marcus Aurelius, were encamped in Sabaste, Armenia, when the Emperor Licinius gave orders that all his armies would sacrifice to the gods. Lysias was their general and Agricola the governor of the province when the order came through.

A delegation from the forty soldiers bravely informed the governor that because they were Christians they would not sacrifice to false gods, and there was nothing he could do to make them abandon their holy religion.

The governor pleaded with them to change their minds, pointing out the dishonour they would bring on the famous Legion. He made generous promises of preferential treatment for them if they would sacrifice.

To his promises they replied that he could give them nothing to compare with what he would deprive them of in eternity.

When the governor's promises turned into threats they retorted that his power only extended over their bodies, which they had learned to despise when their souls were at stake. The governor, finding them resolute, ordered them to be whipped and their sides torn with iron hooks. They were then put into chains and committed to prison.

Days went by and eventually Lysias, their general returned to Sebaste but he fared no better than the governor when he examined the prisoners. All his persuasions failed.

The governor was deeply offended by the courage and eloquence with which they had accosted him. He devised an extraordinary death for them, slow and severe, by which he hoped to shake their constancy.

The cold in Armenia is severe, especially towards the end of winter with the winds blowing from the north and the frosts hard. Near the walls of the town there was a pond, frozen solid; the governor ordered the soldiers to be stripped and exposed on the ice, and in order to tempt them more forcibly to renounce their faith, a warm bath was placed at the edge of the pond.

The soldiers, hearing their sentence, ran joyfully to the pond and without waiting to be stripped, flung off their clothes, shouting and encouraging each other as if they were going into battle and reminding themselves that one bad night would purchase a happy eternity.

They also made a joint prayer: 'Lord, we are forty who are engaged in this combat. Grant that forty may be crowned and that not one be wanting from this sacred number.'

The guards continued to persuade them to give in, the warm bath steamed invitingly, the soldiers grew colder, frozen. Then one of the soldiers gave in. He ran from the frozen pond towards the warm bath and died as he flung himself into the water.

The soldiers agonising in the cold were dispirited, but they were quickly comforted. One of the guards warming himself by the bath suddenly had a vision of blessed spirits descending from heaven on the soldiers. Overcome by the celestial vision, he tore off his clothes to join the other thirty-nine on the ice. God had heard their request and granted it, but in a way they had not expected.

The morning came and the governor ordered a fire to be prepared and those who were still alive cast into it. The bodies were sorted and while some were being thrown into wagons to be carried to the fire, Melito, the youngest of them was found to be more alive than the others. The guards, hoping he would submit if he recovered, left him behind.

But the mother of Melito, a poor widow who had watched all night with anguish, was a woman rich in the faith and worthy to have a son a martyr. She abused the guards for the false compassion they had shown for her son, lying frozen, unable to move and scarcely breathing.

Melito looked up at her and with a weak hand he tried to comfort her. His mother exhorted him to persevere to the end and, fortified by the Holy Spirit, she picked him up and placed him on the wagon with the rest of the martyrs – without shedding a tear. With an expression full of joy she cried out: 'Go my son! Proceed to the end of this happy journey with your companions that you may be with them when they present themselves before the Almighty God.'

Their bodies were burned and the ashes and bones thrown into the river. Eventually their fellow Christians carried their relics away. St Emmelia built a church for them near Anneses and the remains of the gallant forty martyrs were the cause of many miracles.

Unlike the soldiers on the ice, few of us are called to martyrdom. Yet we are all called daily to fight the good fight against our passions and spiritual enemies. To win, or to fight as well as we are able.

St Thomas à Beckett
(1170)
December 29

Thomas à Beckett was born in London on 21 December 1117. His father, Gilbert Beckett was a gentleman but not particularly wealthy, who in his youth had made a pilgrimage to Jerusalem. Captured by the Saracens, he was made a prisoner along with his companions and held as a slave to the Emir, a Muslim ruler, for a year and a half. One day, the Emir's only daughter heard him explain the Christian faith, declaring that his greatest joy would be to lay down his life for God. She was so touched by his love for God that she desired to be a Christian, and told Gilbert. He replied that he would be happy if she did but he warned her that it could cost her dearly.

Gilbert and his fellow slaves one night made their escape and returned to London; the Emir's daughter followed him and was baptised Maud. She was then married to Gilbert at St Paul's Church by the Bishop of London. Soon after, Gilbert went back to the East to join the Crusades and there he remained for three and a half years.

Thomas was born a year after the marriage; his mother brought him up to fear God and inspired him with a tender devotion to the Virgin Mary. His father, after his return from the Crusades became Sheriff of London and placed Thomas in a monastery for his education. Sadly, his father died in 1138 but Thomas continued in the monastery till the age of twenty-one.

After his mother died he abandoned his studies for a year before resuming them at Oxford then in Paris where he studied diligently, chiefly Canon Law. After returning to London he went to live with a noble family in the country, only to be captivated by hunting and hawking and other pursuits. It would appear that he did not keep the best of company until an accident opened his eyes to his failings.

One day, in the pursuit of game, his hawk swooped on a duck but missed and went into the water. Thomas, fearing that he would lose the hawk leapt into the river to rescue it, but a strong current carried him downstream towards a mill. He was saved from certain death when the mill wheel suddenly and miraculously stopped for no apparent reason. In gratitude for his divine deliverance, Thomas resolved to return to London and embark on a more serious and meaningful way of life.

It would seem that Thomas was guided by Theobald, the Archbishop of Canterbury who was an old friend of his late father. At his suggestion, Thomas went to Italy to study Canon Law at Bologna, then at Auxerre. On his return the Archbishop ordained him deacon and after various appointments the Archbishop nominated him Archdeacon of Canterbury, which gave him a seat in the House of Lords.

Thomas was now the Archbishop's trusted helper and adviser. The Archbishop rarely did anything without asking his advice and several times sent him to Rome on important Church affairs. Such was the Archbishop's faith and trust in Thomas that he recommended him to the high office of Lord Chancellor of England. Henry

II, who had ascended to the throne on 20 December 1155, agreed and Thomas was appointed Lord Chancellor in 1157.

The new Lord Chancellor grew in esteem and affection, his virtue and abilities enhancing his reputation. The king committed his son Prince Henry to his care and education, and sent Thomas to France where he successfully concluded a treaty and negotiated a marriage between the Prince and Margaret, the daughter of Louis the Younger, the King of France. Yet amidst his triumphs, honours and prosperity, Thomas lived humbly and mortified, modest and chaste despite the temptations of the Court and the snares of even the king himself.

Theobald died in 1160. King Henry, who was then in Normandy with Thomas, informed him that he was to be the next Archbishop of Canterbury. Thomas replied, 'Should God permit me to accept, I fear I should soon lose your majesty's favour and the great affection with which you honour me would soon turn to hatred.'

Thomas was reluctant to take up the appointment and only did so on the orders of the Cardinal of Pisa, legate from the Holy See in England .

Thomas took up his duties with humility. Next to his skin he wore a hair shirt and over it the habit of a Benedictine monk. He began his day at two o'clock in the morning: he prayed and read the Scriptures, washed the feet of poor people, said Mass then distributed alms to those in need.

But Thomas offended the king by resigning as Chancellor, and further offended by objecting to the king usurping the revenues of the Church. Thomas also curbed the judges, officials and noblemen who oppressed the Church or its lands, and they complained to the king. There were also differences about other financial matters and the king's resentment grew. There were differences about customs of the kingdom, abuses and injustice, oppression of the Church – the king was enraged and he threatened the life of Thomas.

At an assembly of bishops and noblemen at Northampton on 8 October 1164, the king ordered that all Thomas' possessions should be confiscated. Several bishops urged Thomas to resign as Archbishop of Canterbury, but he answered that to do so would betray the truth and the cause of the Church. Rather than do that he would lay down his life

The persecutions increased; his reply was silence, peace and love for his enemies, yet he decided to go abroad for a time. He landed on the continent in 1164 stayed at the abbey of St Bertins at St Omer and the King of France offered him the hospitality of his kingdom. The Pope was at that time in Sens, in France when bishops and envoys arrived there to publicly accuse Thomas before his holiness.

When Thomas arrived at Sens he met with a cold reception from the cardinals and other dignitaries. In an audience with the Pope, Thomas expressed his grief at the injustices to the Church in England and of his desire to secure true peace. His discourse was so moving that even the cardinals approved, and the Pope encouraged him to constancy.

In a second audience the following day, Thomas explained that he had accepted the Archbishopric against his will; then he took the ring from his finger and gave it to the Pope in token of his resignation. After long deliberation the Pope summoned him to return, gave back his ring with the order not to abandon his charge, for that would be to abandon the cause of God. He delivered Thomas into the care of the abbot of Pontigni, to live as a Cistercian monk.

Thomas regarded the austere monastery with delight, and increased his mortifications while submitting himself to all the rules of the Order. King Henry was furious that the pope had supported the Archbishop, and confiscated the belongings of all the friends and relations of Thomas. The Pope tried to bring about a reconciliation, but as the king had threatened to abolish the Order of the Cistercians in England because they had harboured him, Thomas prepared to leave Pontigni. Before he left he was praying before the altar when he heard a voice say, 'Thomas, my Church shall be glorified in your blood.'

Thomas asked, 'Who are you?'

The same voice replied, 'I am Jesus Christ, the Son of the living God, your brother.'

He left Pontigni and arrived in Sens to live in the monastery of St Columba under the protection of the King of France. Here he excommunicated all those who had obeyed the orders of the King of England in seizing the estates of the Church; he also threatened the king himself and exhorted him to repentance.

To undermine the authority of Thomas, Henry ordered the Archbishop of York to crown his son king at Canterbury. Yet suddenly there was a reconciliation, the king asking that their former differences should be buried so they could live in perfect friendship. At Tours, the king promised to restore the treasures of the Church, but he also allowed the Archbishop of York who had been plotting against Thomas to plunder goods from the Church and the harvest of the year.

Nevertheless Thomas resolved to return to England, having been absent for seven years. He was received with great joy when he landed at Sandwich, after escaping several ambush attempts on the road which led him to suspect he was heading for martyrdom. The Archbishop of York demanded absolution from his censures; Thomas agreed to do this providing he acted in accordance with the custom of the Church. The Archbishop refused and went over to Normandy with other bishops to accuse Thomas before King Henry with lies and slander.

The king was enraged and cried out, cursing all those who enjoyed his patronage and friendship but who didn't have the courage to rid him of this troublesome priest. Among those who listened were four young courtiers – Sir William Tracy, Sir Reginald Fitz-Orson, Sir Hugh Morville, Sir Richard Briton – and they conspired to murder Thomas.

It was in the cathedral at Canterbury where they found him, at the hour of vespers. The knights entered, sword in hand asking, 'Where is the traitor?' No one answered. Someone asked, 'Where is the Archbishop?'

Thomas appeared, calm and serene. One of the knights exclaimed, 'Now you must die!'

Thomas answered, 'I am ready to die for God, for justice and for the liberty of the Church but I forbid you to harm any of the clergy or people.' He fell to his knees and said, 'I recommend my soul and the cause of the Church to God, to the Blessed Virgin, to the holy saints of this place and to the martyrs St Dionysius and St Elphege of Canterbury.'

They tried to take him out from the church but Thomas refused to go. The knights, afraid of interference from the people who had crowded in, decided to act fast. Tracy struck at the head of Thomas but one of the clergy, Edward Grim tried to protect the Archbishop with his arm, which was almost cut off. Two of the knights swung their swords and Thomas fell down before the altar of St Benedict. Richard Briton took his turn to cut off part of the head of Thomas and in doing so broke his sword on the ground. Then Hugh of Horsea stuck his sword into the head, scattering the saint's brains on the floor. After they had completed their despicable act they attacked the archiepiscopal palace with fury and passion.

Canterbury was a sea of remorse, grief and tears. A blind man recovered his sight at the touch of the martyr's still warm blood. The doors of the cathedral were locked, and the body of the saint quickly interred the next day, because it was rumoured that the murderers were going to drag it through the streets.

St Thomas was martyred on 29 December 1170 at the age of fifty-three.

There was widespread sorrow and grief among all the Catholic monarchs and princes of Christendom and in the hearts of the people. King Henry forgot his animosity and abandoned the dignity of his crown to bewail his sins in sackcloth and ashes. He shut himself away for a three day fast and spent the next forty days crying and wailing in grief. He sent envoys to the Pope assuring him that he had never commanded nor desired this foul murder; the Pope excommunicated the assassins.

The king was a true penitent and a changed man. He abolished the customs and abuses which had come between him and Thomas, restoring all the church lands and revenues he had usurped. His conversion and the cures of lepers, the blind and the deaf were regarded as the result of the martyrdom of Thomas; even the dead were restored to life. But God punished King Henry. His son rebelled against him, supported by most of the nobility and the King of Scotland. Henry made a pilgrimage to the tomb of Thomas and walked the last three miles over rough stones, leaving his feet cut and blooded. A whole day and a night he prayed, and the next morning he was informed his men had captured the King of Scotland. Soon after, Henry's son begged and received his pardon.

The four murderers shut themselves up in the house of one of them, Hugh of Morville in the west of England, filled with remorse and shunned by all. Later, they travelled to Rome to receive absolution from the Pope; at his suggestion they made a pilgrimage to Jerusalem where three of them lived and died as true penitents in a place called Montenigro. They were buried at the gate of the Church of Jerusalem with the inscription: *Here lieth the wretches who martyred blessed Thomas, Archbishop of Canterbury.*

The remaining knight who had struck the first blow went to Cosenza in Calabria to commence his penance, and there he died with the flesh rotting on his bones.

All four murderers died within three years of the martyrdom of the saint.

St Hippolytus

(AD 252)

August 13

Hippolytus was one of the twenty-five priests of Rome who suffered under the reign of Gallus. For a time he had followed the schismatic teachings of Novation and Novatus. He then made amends for this grievous error with an act of public repentance, but he was arrested and tortured on the rack in the city of Rome. The prefect of that city went to Ostia to extend the persecution and he ordered that Hippolytus and other Christians should be taken with him. Hippolytus had a farewell message for those who begged his advice before he was taken to Ostia: 'Return to the Catholic Church. Cling to the faith which was preached by Paul and maintained by the chair of Peter. I now see things in a different light and regret what I once taught.'

The prefect ascended the tribunal surrounded by his executioners and various instruments of torture, the Christians ranged before him, dirty, filthy and emaciated after their long months in prison. Yet not one of them would deny the Faith and all of them were condemned to death. Some were beheaded, others crucified or burnt, the rest were put out to sea in rotting vessels and so they were drowned.

It was now the turn of Hippolytus and he was brought before the prefect loaded with chains. A crowd of young people gathered and cried out that because he was the leader of the Christians, he should be put to death by some new and unusual torment.

'What is your name?' the prefect asked.

'Hippolytus,' was the reply.

The prefect considered, then said, 'Then you shall die like Hippolytus!' By this the prefect alluded to Hippolytus the son of Theseus of Greek legend who, while fleeing from the anger of his father, met a monster which so frightened the horses that he fell from his chariot, became entangled in the harness and was torn to pieces.

As soon as the sentence was pronounced the executioners, assisted by the people, set to work searching the countryside to capture two wild horses. They roped the feet of Hippolytus to each of the animals then whipped them hard so they galloped furiously away and into the woods. Through ditches and streams they dragged him, through bushes and hedges, over rough ground and rocks, leaving a trail of blood and mangled flesh and limbs.

The Christians who had witnessed the martyrdom of Hippolytus with tears of respect and admiration managed to gather up the remains of his noble body. They were taken to Rome and buried in the catacombs, where prayers in honour of the martyr were said and requests for the infirmities of body and soul were granted.

He died on 13 August 252.

St Joseph of Cupertino

(1603-1663)

September 18

Joseph Desa's parents were so poor that he was born in a garden shed! The place was Cupertino, a small village between Brindisi and Otranto in Italy and the date of his birth was 17 June 1603. They were miserably poor because his father's business had failed, so they had to sell the family home – the penalty for being so heavily in debt. His mother resented the little Joseph, who was a backward child, sickly, pale and very thin; he caught every disease that came his way and once he almost died. In her heart his mother thought it might be for the best if her son *did* die: there was no hope for the stupid child, he was just another burden for her to carry.

His teachers and school soon gave up on him and the other children made fun of his pigeon-toes and called him 'Boccaperta' (the Gaper) because his mouth always hung open. His mother soon realised that he was wasting his time at school so she took him to a shoemaker to be his apprentice. But Joseph was not a success as a shoemaker; he had neither the ability nor the concentration and so, at the age of seventeen he began to think about finding something he could do successfully.

One day, a monk came into the shop to buy leather and tallow. The monk set Joseph thinking and he decided he would like to be a monk and maybe for once in his life could be of help to others. Joseph asked permission from his mother to leave shoemaking and enter a monastery. His mother was delighted and willingly agreed, so Joseph went to a monastery of the Conventual Franciscans where two of his uncles were distinguished members of the Order, but he was rejected as being academically unsuitable. He was rejected by many other monasteries until eventually the Franciscans at La Grotella gave him work as a stable boy.

Joseph was still determined to become a monk and his prayers were answered when his austere life of penance, humility and obedience could no longer be ignored, and he was accepted as a lay brother. What he lacked academically he made up for by his dedication and devotion to acquire a spirit-infused knowledge, which enabled him to solve the most intricate theological questions. He also possessed the gifts of prophecy and healing. He could easily recognise sinners because their faces appeared black to him, and so even though he could barely read he was ordained priest at the age of twenty-five in 1628.

For the next five years the devout Joseph declined bread and wine and existed only on herbs and dried fruit. He kept Lent with severe mortifications.

It was shortly after he became a priest that another divine gift emerged and his extraordinary levitations began. He flew on innumerable occasions and it is recorded that he once helped builders in the monastery by lifting a huge cross to a height of thirty-six feet and then stayed perched on it for several hours. Others have had the gift of levitation but Joseph took it to a fine art. He only had to think about God and he would rise up into the air.

This usually happened in church where he would circle high above the altar and there he would stay until mass had finished. His levitations could happen at any time, anywhere and occasionally he would take off during meal times with a dish of food in his hands, much to the alarm of the other friars. If he was outdoors he would soar up into a tree the slightest hint of devotion and up he would go.

It is reputed that he once conversed and prayed with sheep, that he cured a blind boy by simply touching his eyes, that he held the hand of a dying child and the child recovered instantly. Incredible gifts were bestowed by Almighty God on this holy man who carried in his heart the priceless treasure of profound humility. The troubles of this life he called 'the war of children with pop guns', and obedience 'the carriage to Paradise'.

Joseph's fame as a 'flyer' spread, and it is said to have reached the ears of the Spanish ambassador. He arrived at the monastery to investigate this strange phenomenon, but when Joseph entered the church he flew right over the heads of the ambassador's entourage, to the foot of his favourite image of the Virgin Mary. There he remained for a time before flying back over them again.

Joseph loved Christmas, especially the carols. As soon as they began he would fly straight up, still in a kneeling position, and would remain high in the air until the carols had finished. But the supernatural happenings to Joseph were a source of constant embarrassment to the Church authorities and they grew increasingly disturbed. He was accused of 'drawing crowds like a new Messiah' so he was hidden away in seclusion, yet the devout and the curious continued to seek him out however much the authorities moved him.

Controversy continued to surround this humble man with the amazing gift of levitation, this man of mortification who kept seven 'Lents' a year. Yet his superior called him a hypocrite, treated him with the utmost severity and ordered him to retire to the convent at Assisi. Here Joseph suffered many trials... and fell into a state of deep melancholia. God again smiled on him and his depression lifted, only for him to be taken ill at Ostia and it was here he died on 18 September 1663, a month after his last flight.

Not surprisingly, he is the patron saint of aviators.

Blessed Nicholas Owen
(AD 1606)

It could be said of Nicholas Owen, the humble and secret Jesuit lay brother, that few did more to preserve the Catholic Faith in England during those horrific penal times following the Reformation.

A builder by trade, between 1580 and 1606, through danger and treachery, he travelled all over England constructing ingenious hiding holes for religious who were being hunted like vermin by the merciless priest hunters. He was both architect and builder, and examples of his unique craft were displayed at Hindlip Hall (Worcestershire), Harrowden (Northampton), Sawston Hall (Cambridge), Broadoaks (Essex) and it is almost certain that he worked at Harvington Hall (Worcestershire) where its cunning priest holes can still be found today. Secret passages, a dummy fireplace for an emergency exit, huge beams in walls that swung open to provide hidden sanctuary, hiding places among the rafters in the roof, fake chimneys, a hinged staircase which lifted to reveal a secure place of concealment – all the work of a genius and every 'hide' unique.

Owen worked in total secrecy, alone and often through the night, breaking into walls, excavating, heaving huge stones even though he was small in stature (he was known as Little John). Before he commenced any project he always received Holy Communion then accompanied his work with prayer, to inspire him to create his masterpieces of subterfuge.

For a time he was a servant to Fr Edmund Campion, but after the renowned Jesuit was arrested, Owen spoke so warmly of him in public that he himself was arrested and imprisoned in the Counter. Here he was tortured incessantly in an attempt to make him reveal the whereabouts of priests, but he said nothing. Eventually a certain Catholic gentleman paid over a sum of money and he was released. He then became a servant to Fr John Gerrard yet he and his master were betrayed by one of the many traitors so it was back to the Counter again for Owen, but again he was released for money.

After his release he helped in the escape of Fr Gerrard from the Tower of London and he was then employed by Fr Henry Garnet, the Jesuit Provincial. When the so-called 'Gunpowder Plot' was discovered, Fr Garnet and Br Owen were implicated and sought refuge at Hindlip Hall. Betrayal was rife and betrayed they were, but when Mr Justice Bromley arrived at the Hall with one hundred armed men, Fr Garnet and a Fr Oldcorn (who also happened to be there) slipped into one of the hiding holes and Owen into another.

The priest hunters searched for a week but with no success and Owen, fearing that the priests would die of starvation gave himself up, hoping to be taken for Fr Garnet. It didn't work. The hunters violently renewed their efforts and spent the next five days stripping panelling and breaking through walls till eventually they discovered the two priests who had been in hiding for almost two weeks.

Br Owen was taken to the Tower of London where he was tortured with a variety of evil devices for six days to make him reveal his hiding places, yet the only words he uttered were, 'Jesus' and 'Mary'. He was already suffering from a hernia and the torture was making it worse, so to keep him alive until he confessed they fixed an iron band around his stomach. He was strung up with iron manacles around his wrists then weights were hung on his feet... more weights... till eventually his bowels burst.

Br Nicholas Owen died in terrible agony and so passed to his eternal reward, this little man with the big, brave heart. Yet his spirit will forever abide in those concealed rooms and secret passages, the hinged staircases and swinging beams.

St Maria Goretti
(1890-1902)

In this modern, enlightened and permissive age, the virtue of holy purity is hard to find, buried by society under a pile of degradation. A hundred years ago, the defence of this precious virtue cost a little girl her life.

Maria Goretti was born on 16 October 1890 at Corinaldo, Italy, the second daughter of Luigi and Assunta Goretti: an unremarkable couple, humble peasants and quite illiterate, yet remarkable for their deep faith which they had passed on to their children. Angelo was the eldest; there were two younger brothers Alessandro and Mariano, and two sisters, Ersilia and Teresa. The family worked hard in the fields trying to scratch a living from the poor soil, Maria and her brothers and sisters contributing as best they could with Maria taking the added responsibility of looking after the baby.

The poverty of the soil eventually forced the Goretti family to leave the district, finally settling at Ferriere de Conca near Nettuno, a seaside town thirty miles west of Rome. Economic circumstances (which would later prove to be tragic) forced them to share a house with Giovanni Serenelli and his teenage son Alessandro.

Though education was compulsory in Italy, it would appear that Maria never went to school, probably because she was needed to contribute to the family budget. Yet she was a sensible little girl, well-informed, devout in her faith with a tender devotion to Our Lord and his Blessed Mother. The death of her father on 6 May 1900 was a great sorrow for her and a disaster for the family.

The presence of Giovanni Serenelli and his son in the house was proving to be most uncomfortable, even menacing. Giovanni was constantly drunk and in trouble with the police, his son obsessed with sex and obscenities. But the Goretti family were stuck with them, not having the money to move away. So Assunta, at the age of thirty-six was left a widow with six children, the eldest twelve and the youngest three months. The future looked decidedly troubled.

The brooding menace of the Serenellis had increased with the death of the father Luigi. Giovanni propositioned Assunta and Alessandro cast lustful eyes on Maria, now in her twelfth year, and began to pester her. Maria rejected his unwanted attentions and began to avoid him at every opportunity. Alessandro made an attempt to assault her and when she fought him off he threatened to kill her if she told anyone.

Maria was now responsible for all the domestic work in the family while her mother took Luigi's place in the fields. She was up at dawn to work and pray all day and finally, in the light of an oil lamp she would mend the worn clothes of the family. She begged to make her first Holy Communion, but Maria was too young. Yet she persisted so much that eventually she did make her first Holy Communion, on 16 June 1901. Neighbours contributed everything: someone lent white shoes, another gave a candle, a veil and someone else a dark red dress with white spots for the great occasion. Maria offered her first Holy Communion, with her prayers for the soul of her dead father.

Everyday life went on as usual, Assunta and some of the children working in the fields with the two Serenellis. Alessandro continued to watch Maria, to lust after her; he tried flattery but quickly realised that it wasn't going to work. Then one afternoon in June 1902 Maria was surprised to see Alessandro returning to the house, and there he tried to assault her again. Maria told no one but she did ask her mother not to leave her alone with Alessandro. Assunta comforted her by telling her that soon he would be called up for military service, yet she never once suspected that her eleven years old daughter was in sexual danger.

On the morning of 5 July 1902, Maria and her friend Teresa Cimarelli made plans to go to church the next day for Mass and Holy Communion, and Maria seemed to be much happier. Outside, in the blazing sunshine, work went on as usual; inside, Maria began her work then later she sat at the top of the stairs to mend a shirt and watch the children. Suddenly, Alessandro came in through the door, ran up the stairs past Maria and into a storeroom. There he found an implement with a long blade which Luigi had bought to sew and repair brooms. He shouted to Maria to come into the storeroom but when she refused, he dragged her in. Despite the fact that people were working close by outside, no one heard her cries for help; the noise of the threshing machine made sure of that.

Once again Alessandro tried to assault her, once again little Maria fought him off. He threatened her with the long blade, but still she refused his demands. Frustrated and in a frenzy he began to stab her, driving the blade into her again and again, stabbing and slashing like a man possessed with evil. Maria cried out again, calling for her mother for help: 'Please come, Alessandro is killing me!'

Alessandro panicked. He grabbed her round the throat then finally stabbed her in the back. He threw the weapon behind a piece of furniture then he went into his own room, locking the door behind him; he lay on his bed and pretended to be asleep.

By this time the baby was crying loudly. Assunta heard the baby's cries and, surprised that there was no Maria, she began to feel uneasy. It was Giovanni who found Maria and he gave the alarm. He told Assunta that Maria had said that Alessandro had murdered her. 'Your Alessandro, not mine.'

Assunta thought differently, since her Alessandro was only seven years old. Maria's friend Teresa helped Assunta to lift the blood-stained young girl on to a bed and when they asked her what had happened, she explained: 'It was Alessandro. He wanted to do bad things to me but when I refused he stabbed me all over.'

The police were called and then an ambulance. News of the tragedy spread like wildfire and soon an angry crowd gathered at the farmhouse. The bloodstained weapon was found, then it was realised that Alessandro was still in the farmhouse. Workers began banging on his door and eventually smashed it open. Feelings were running high but luckily for Alessandro the police were there and he was taken to Nettuno, with the mob hurling stones and screaming, 'Death! Death! Death!' all the way to the jail.

The local doctor arrived but he could do little for Maria. An hour later, a horsedrawn ambulance came to take her, with her mother and Teresa the eight miles over the rough roads to Nettuno, a journey that took four hours. Maria eventually arrived at the hospital of St John of God, but due to the seriousness of her injuries she was unable to be given even a little water. The doctors decided it was hopeless; there were fourteen stab wounds and all her internal organs had been damaged. In terrible pain, Maria did not die, saying over and over again, 'Poor Alessandro. He is going to hell... going to hell...' Her concern for her vile assailant was truly amazing.

The parish priest of Nettuno came to see her. He spoke to her of Our Lord's death on the cross and the forgiveness of his murderers. Would she forgive Alessandro? Maria said she forgave him with all her heart then, for only the fifth time in her life she received Holy Communion.

Weak and close to death she became delirious, and relived the horrific attack of the previous afternoon time and time again. She begged her mother not to let Alessandro near her and cried out, 'What are you doing, Alessandro? No. No! You'll go to hell!' She tried to struggle out of bed to escape the nightmare, but she fell back dead. It was the afternoon of 6 July 1902.

Her body now rests at Nettuno in the church which is dedicated to her.

After his arrest, Alessandro still maintained he was innocent. He was indignant and outraged that he had been accused and he denied knowing anything about it. At his trial in Rome on what would have been Maria's twelfth birthday he showed no remorse, accepted no blame but when the evidence against him proved to be overwhelming he finally admitted his guilt – but pleaded insanity. Because he was a minor he could not be executed or sentenced to life imprisonment, so instead he was sentenced to thirty years in jail.

For many long years Alessandro remained defiant, but one night, after he had been in prison for eight years, he had a dream. He was in a garden and he saw Maria wearing a white dress and picking lilies. She collected a large bunch and offered them to him; he took them from her and it was then he knew she had forgiven him. After this, he was a changed man.

Bishop Blandini in a visit reminded Alessandro of the mercy of God and his forgiveness of even the gravest sins. Alessandro repented and became a model prisoner then after twenty-six years he was released from his prison in Sardinia. It took him eight years to save enough money to return to Italy and the first thing he did was to visit the tomb of Maria. He then went to the presbytery at Corinaldo where Assunta was housekeeper to beg her forgiveness. She answered that as Maria had forgiven him she could not refuse. As it was Christmas, Assunta asked permission from the priest for Alessandro to stay for a few days and at Midnight Mass in the year 1937, they received Holy Communion together.

Alessandro went to an isolated monastery and

worked as a gardener until his death at the age of eighty-two in 1969. His last words were, 'I am going to be with Maria.'

The story of Maria Goretti is a lesson in ultimate forgiveness, a lesson in profound repentance and an example of God's love which conquers all.

Maria was declared saint on 24 June 1950.

St James Intercisus

(5th century)
November 27

James Intercisus was a native of Persia, now known as Iran. He was also a Christian, a nobleman, courtier and a highly esteemed friend of King Isdegerdes. When the king began to persecute the Christians, James had not the courage to resist and rather than lose the king's favour and patronage, he abandoned his worship of the one true God.

His mother and his wife were saddened by his behaviour and when the king died they wrote a letter to James: 'We were told a long time ago that you had forsaken the love of God for the sake of the king's favour and the riches of this world. Look now where the king lies, he is but dust, the fate of all mortals. You can no longer expect any patronage from him and neither can he protect you from eternal torment. If you continue to renounce the one true God, you yourself will receive Divine Justice with your friend, the king.'

James was deeply upset when he read this letter from those he loved so much; he began to reflect on his life and came to a decision. He appeared no more at court, shunned his new-found friends and the pleasures, pomp and honours which had seduced him from his God. He became a true penitent, an outspoken penitent and his words were quickly carried to the new king who immediately commanded his presence before him.

King Vararanes furiously denounced James for his ingratitude to his royal master for the many favours and honours he had received.

James boldly confessed to being a Christian and calmly said, 'Where is your father, the old king now? He is but dust.'

The quiet words of James infuriated the tyrant. He threatened that his punishment would not be a speedy death but a lingering torment.

James replied: 'Any death is but a sleep.'

'Death,' said the king, 'is not sleep, it is the terror of lords and kings.'

'It does indeed terrify those who refuse to accept the one true God. The wicked shall perish.'

'You call us wicked!' the king screamed.

'I do not accuse you,' James replied. 'But do not give the name God to the creatures and idols which you worship.'

The wrath of the king was fearful to behold. He called together his ministers and advisers so they could deliberate on what new kind of cruel death they could devise for the notorious James.

After long deliberation they reached a conclusion. If James would not renounce Christ, he would be hung up on a rack and his limbs cut off one by one, joint by joint. As soon as the sentence was made public, the whole city flocked to see this unique execution. Meanwhile, the Christians prayed to God that James would persevere until death.

When James arrived at the place of execution, he fell down on his knees, lifted up his eyes to heaven and prayed with great fervour while the executioners made ready with a display of scimitars and other instruments of torture. They explained to him the cruel death he was going to suffer and tried to cajole him into obeying the king. The heathens in the crowd also tried to persuade him to submit by saying he could renounce his religion for the time being and return to it afterwards.

James answered, 'This death I am about to endure is but a cheap price to pay for the rewards of eternal life.' He then said to the executioners, 'Do not stand idle. Begin your work.'

They tied him onto a rack, stretched out his arm and cut off his right thumb.

James prayed aloud: 'O Saviour of Christians, receive a branch from the tree, but it will bud again and, as I believe, I shall be clothed in glory.'

The Judge who had been appointed by the king to oversee the execution burst into tears, as did many who were watching. They cried out: 'You have lost much for the sake of your religion. Do not die this way.'

James replied, 'The vine dies in winter yet it revives in the spring. My body which is cut down shall live again.'

When his first finger was cut off he cried aloud: 'Receive, O Lord, another branch.' The joy in his heart seemed to be greater than the pain he suffered and that joy shone out from his face.

As each finger was cut off he rejoiced and thanked God. All the fingers on his right hand... then all the fingers on his left. The Judge entreated him to think again.

James answered meekly, 'He is not worthy of God

who, after putting his hand to the plough shall look back.'

The big toe on his right foot was cut off... the other toes, then all the toes on his left foot. Now all his fingers and toes were gone he cheerfully said to the executioners, 'Now the boughs are gone, cut down the trunk. Do not pity me for my heart rejoices in the Lord and my soul is lifted up to him.'

They cut off his right foot, then the left. His right hand and then his left hand. Right arm, and left. His right leg and then the left.

As he lay trembling on the ground in his own blood, his thighs were torn from the hips. Yet lying there, a naked trunk and having lost half his body he still cheerfully prayed and praised God till a guard crowned his martyrdom by severing his head from his body.

His execution took place on 27 November 421, the second year of the reign of King Vararanes.

The Christians offered a large sum of money for the relics of St James. They were not allowed to redeem them but later, when the opportunity arose, they carried them away. They found twenty-eight pieces and these they placed in a chest together with the congealed blood which they had soaked up with linen cloths.

It is said that some of his blood had been taken up by the sun, so its rays tinged the limbs of the martyr a glorious red.

The Four Blessed Sisters of Charity at Arras
(AD 1794)
June 26

The reign of terror in France was at its height, yet the Sisters of Charity at Arras continued to work among the sick and the poor in the town, loved and venerated by all. The situation became desperate, then dangerous, so Sr Madeleine Fontaine the Superior decided to send the two youngest Sisters of the Order into Belgium for their own safety, leaving Sisters Marie Laval, Therese Fanton and Jean Gerrard to help her in the works of mercy.

The good sisters suffered much. They were deprived of the Mass and the Sacraments, cut off from the Mother House and harassed in all kinds of cruel ways by the Republican fanatics. They were also called upon to take the *Oath of Liberté, Egalité et Confraternité* which denied ecclesiastical authority. The four Sisters courageously refused, so on 15 February 1794 they were arrested.

The 'Terror' was rampant in Arras under the direction of 'Citizen' Joseph Lebon, once a priest; he had filled the jails with aristocrats and peasants alike and many were sent to the guillotine without trial. His so-called wife, Mimi, a disgusting woman of ill repute encouraged him in the atrocities and took a leading part. She would watch all day from a balcony, gloating and jeering as the victims were dragged to their deaths.

The four sisters remained in prison at Arras and during those four long months they stayed cheerful and resolute, determined not to be afraid of the terror of the situation. In May 1794 Lebon and his cohorts moved the guillotine to Cambrai where he ordered the church bells to be rung to welcome the 'Red Widow'. School children were ordered to watch the executions: 'The fall of the apricots!' cackled the sadistic Mimi.

The daily executions at Arras alone had exceeded two thousand and now the guillotine was in full flow again at Cambrai. Such was its mesmerising effect on the children that some of them had toy guillotines to play with, to execute birds and small mammals.

The following month the Sisters were taken to Cambrai. They cheerfully accepted that this was a summons to death and arriving at the Court they again refused to take the obnoxious oath. Sentence of death was passed and they were condemned to the guillotine. It was market day and through the bustling crowds and bright sunshine these heroic Sisters were taken to their deaths.

Standing erect on the bloody scaffold, the gallant Superior watched and while waiting her own turn to suffer she cried out: 'Christians, listen. We are the last victims. The persecution will cease and the altars of Jesus will be restored.'

Her prophecy proved to be correct. That night, the infamous Lebon was summoned to Paris on terrorist business and though he eventually returned to Cambrai it was after the fall of Robespierre and the end of the 'Terror' – the terror which had engulfed France for over a year and was at least the equal in its atrocities to anything history had to offer.

The Jesuit Martyrs of Canada

(1642-1649)
June 21

The name Canada is said to be derived from the Indian word 'Kannatha', a collection of huts or a village. It was in the region of Quebec under the rule of the French Governor Champlain (1615-1635) that the Catholic missions made great strides in this vast, uncharted territory.

Franciscan and Jesuit Fathers made the long and perilous voyage across the Atlantic in boats that looked like giant coal scuttles and were about as stable as corks bobbing in the sea. Arrival was not guaranteed, but arrive they did and travelled far into this wild and rugged country, preaching chiefly among the Hurons, the Algonquins and the Iroquois – fierce Indian tribes who had little time or respect for gentle Christianity. These nomadic Indians, particularly the Iroquois resented the efforts of the missionaries to settle them in the villages. Inter-tribal wars, massacres and diabolical vengeance all combined to make the spreading of the Gospel extremely difficult and dangerous.

The first missionary to die for the faith was Br Rene Goupil on 2 August 1642. The next month, Fr Isaac Jogues was seized by the Iroquois, but after enduring horrible tortures he managed to escape and returned to Paris. He later came back to continue his work among the Indians; he was killed by the Iroquois in 1646, together with Fr Jean de la Lande.

The other Jesuits who lost their lives in the cause of the Christian Faith were: Fr Antoine Daniel, born at Dieppe in 1601. He was in charge of the Mission of St Joseph with a congregation of about four hundred families, mostly Hurons. On the morning of 14 July as Fr Daniel was saying Mass the village was attacked by the Iroquois and he was among those slain.

Fr Jean de Brebeuf was born at Conde-sur-Vire in 1593. He travelled mostly in a canoe, for many years baptising and evangelising, but he was captured by hostile Indians in March 1649 and subjected to horrifying tortures. His fingernails were torn out, boiling oil was poured over him in a mockery of baptism and finally his heart was torn out.

Fr Gabriel Lalemant, born at Paris in 1610 suffered with him. He was tortured for seventeen hours before his life was ended with a blow from a tomahawk.

In December the same year, Fr Charles Garnier, born in Paris in 1606, was shot down with arrows and axed to death. His friend, Noel Chabanel, born 1613, was put to death the following day.

These are but a few of that glorious band of missionaries who gave their lives for the love of Jesus and the salvation of souls.

Blessed Francis Regis Clet

(1742-1820)

February 18

The holy advice of Our Lord, 'When they persecute you in one city, flee to another,' is easily applied to the heroic life and labours of Francis Regis Clet in the Chinese mission field.

He was born at Grenoble, France on 20 August 1748, the tenth of fifteen children; his father, Cesaire Clet was a prosperous merchant of that city. After completing his course of Humanities at the Jesuit College of Grenoble, the young Francis entered the diocesan seminary, then under the direction of the Oratorian Fathers. His family was devoutly religious, one of his brothers joining the Carthusians while a sister became a Carmelite. In March 1769 Francis enrolled as a novice with the Lazarists, a Congregation founded by St Vincent de Paul. He took his vows in 1770 and three years later he was ordained priest.

The next fifteen years he spent in the obscure but important post of Professor of Moral Theology at Annecy, where his renowned intellect earned him the title of 'The Living Library'. In 1788, Fr Cayla de la Garde was elected as the new Superior General of the Lazarists and one of his first appointments was to nominate Francis as Master of Novices at the Paris House of St Lazare. But in 1789 the French Revolution erupted and in July the House was stormed during the bread riots. It was so badly damaged that both Fathers and novices could not return; in fact they never did and after the Reign of Terror it became a prison for female offenders.

The rapid progress of the Revolution quickly brought matters of Church and state to a crisis. In 1791 Superior General Fr Cayla refused to take the oath of the 'Civil Constitution of the Clergy' and went into exile. About the same time, Fr Clet received permission to join members of the Congregation who were labouring in the far away mission fields of China. Together with two young Lazarists he reached Macao, the Portuguese settlement on the Canton River where he spent several months trying to attain a working knowledge of the Chinese language. The spartan way of life must have come as something of a culture shock to this distinguished academic and he never totally mastered this difficult language consisting of 60,000 characters, representing not sounds but ideas! Yet he became one of the people by adapting native dress, wearing a beard and shaving his head. He lived in a wretched straw hut which he called his 'straw palace' and in the year he spent in Keang Si he baptised about one hundred adults after long and careful instruction in the faith.

In 1793 he placed himself at the disposal of Fr Aubin at Hou-Kouang and this was to be his home for the rest of his life. The centre of the Lazarist mission at that time was at Kucheng, near Lake Tong Tin, with three priests in charge: Frs Aubin, Pesne and Clet. They often had to traverse distances of up to one hundred and fifty miles to care for their scattered flock, partly as a result of the persecution of 1784 which had left an aftermath of fear and dejection. Many of those who

146

remained faithful were still addicted to various heathen practices.

Between 1795 and 1797 Fr Clet's companion priests died and so he had to labour on alone. Ever watchful, he managed to avoid the unwelcome attentions of the marauding bands of mercenaries who were up in arms against the Emperor Kia-King. His native congregation numbered around ten thousand, of whom about two thousand lived close to his 'straw palace'.

He now had the assistance of two Chinese priests but often had to make long missionary journeys which kept him away for months at a time. He visited regions that had not seen a priest in years, catechising, exhorting and administering the Sacraments with true religious zeal, then in 1810 his Lazarist Superiors at Peking gave him the assistance of Fr Dumazel. The next year, owing to false rumours that foreigners in China were plotting to take over the country, the Emperor issued a decree ordering all persons who were not native to leave. Although the decree was later rescinded, much bad feeling had been aroused and in 1812, Fr Clet's 'straw palace', the church and schoolhouse were burned to the ground by an angry mob. Six years later he lost Fr Dumazel, when his faithful assistant died.

Yet the work they had done began to bear fruit. The Christians, by now a numerous body revered their surviving pastor as a living saint, and even the pagans regarded him as a friend of 'the Master of Heaven', but the final trial was now at hand. As in the days of the persecutions under the Roman Emperors, so it now happened to the Christians in China. In May 1818, the Christians were accused not of subversion but

147

of causing by their 'spells' certain atmospheric disturbances, and a severe persecution began.

For a time Fr Clet was concealed by a Christian family at Ho-Nan but eventually he was betrayed by a renegade native Christian in the year 1819. For eight months he was dragged from prison to prison and subjected to various judicial tortures, beaten in the face with leather straps then confined in a wooden cage scarcely able to sit, lie, stand or kneel. On 1 January 1820, Fr Clet and a Chinese priest, Fr Chen were sentenced to death at Hou Pe. The following month the Emperor confirmed the death sentence on Fr Clet for 'deceiving and corrupting' the Chinese people by teaching them the Christian religion.

Early on the morning of 18 February the brave missionary priest was taken outside the walls of the city and there, before an immense crowd, he was bound to a cross and slowly strangled to death. Yet amazingly, the Emperor and all who had contrived the martyr's death, including the renegade who had betrayed him, met with violent deaths within six months of Fr Clet's cruel martyrdom. Even the heathens were impressed by this and some of them remarked: 'See how the persecutors of the Christians have perished!'

The venerable remains of this heroic priest were buried in the Christian cemetery at Ouching-Fu, then in 1868 they were transferred to the Mother House of the Lazarist Order in Paris, to be interred beneath the altar.

St Bernadette

(1844-1879)

February 11

Bernadette is probably one of the most well known and best loved of all the saints. She was born at Lourdes on 7 January 1844 and baptised Marie Bernard the next day, but later she was to be called Bernadette. She was the daughter of Francois Soubirous, a miller who had, through bad management, brought his business to ruin. So the family had to leave the mill on the Lapaca, a strong stream flowing into the River Gave, to live in a building in the Rue des Petits-Fosses once used as the local prison and known as 'the lock-up' (*le cachot*). She was a sickly child with asthma prominent among her other illnesses, so in 1857 she went to live with a family named Aravant at Bartres where she looked after the sheep. While there the local Curé instructed her in the Faith, but she was not happy at Bartres and in the following year got her wish to return to Lourdes where she continued her preparations for her first Holy Communion.

It was after her return to Lourdes on Thursday 11 February on a bitterly cold day that Bernadette went with her sister Toinette and a friend, Jeanne Abardie to gather firewood on the banks of the Gave. Bernadette was left alone when the others wandered off in search of firewood; suddenly she heard a noise like a gust of wind and when she looked up she saw in the grotto of the rock on the opposite bank, the figure of a Lady dressed in white, a veil covering her head. There was a blue sash, a Rosary hanging from her right arm, yellow roses at her feet and the figure was bathed in light. Bernadette was frightened, tried to say the Rosary, couldn't make the sign of the cross, tried again... and this time succeeded.

Her fear passed as she said the Rosary and when she had finished praying the Lady smiled, bowed her head, then disappeared. From a short distance away, the other children could see Bernadette on her knees praying and they laughed at her. 'Did you see anything?' asked Bernadette.

'No,' they replied.

Toinette insisted: 'You were frightened. What did you see?'

Eventually Bernadette told her and made her promise to keep it a secret, but she didn't, and told their mother. 'We must pray,' she said. 'Perhaps it was a soul from Purgatory.' And she forbade them to return to the grotto.

But on Sunday 14 February with her father's permission Bernadette returned to the grotto with her friends and the vision came again, smiling and beautiful. From this time until 18 July of the same year some eighteen manifestations took place, then ceased.

The appearance of the vision on 25 February to Bernadette was particularly significant. Amidst rumours and speculation the news had spread like wildfire and there was a crowd of four to five thousand people watching, eyes searching and seeking, yet seeing nothing when the Lady said to Bernadette, 'Go, drink at the source and wash in it.'

Bernadette turned to drink from the river but the

Lady said she did not mean the river, and pointed her finger to the ground close by. Bernadette could see only a hint of muddy water but she scratched with her fingers and water came, muddy water, then water clear enough to drink and flow...

A month later, on 24 March a statue of Our Lady had been carried in procession to the grotto; carriage-loads of people were coming in from Tarbes to boost the immense crowd already gathering there, yet it was not until the next day that Bernadette went to the grotto to find the vision awaiting her. After a time in ecstasy, Bernadette asked, 'Madame, will you have the goodness to tell me who you are?'

Three times Bernadette asked. After the third request the Lady replied, 'I am the Immaculate Conception.'

The reports of these extraordinary occurrences caused great excitement in the district and the parish priest, the Abbé Pomian and the nuns at the convent who had instructed Bernadette were incredulous. Some people thought that the apparition was the soul of a young girl who had recently died, most people thought that it was some kind of hallucination.

Nevertheless, the huge crowds were persistent and Bernadette was interrogated by the local Commissary and the Imperial Prosecutor. Her replies were humble, straightforward and amazingly intelligent considering she was only a poor peasant girl who could neither read nor write. She had seen a vision of a beautiful young lady, 'lovelier than I have ever seen'.

Time passed, speculation continued but the grotto was closed by the order of Baron Massey, the Prefect of Tarbes on the grounds that the spring which had suddenly appeared had medicinal properties and was therefore government property. The water was analysed and found to have no medicinal properties so by a decree of Napolean III the grotto was re-opened to the public.

On 17 November 1858 Bernadette was again interrogated before a commission authorised by the Bishop of Tarbes, she replied to all the questions with simple and honest answers. After four years of due consideration of the circumstances, the Bishop declared the alleged apparitions had all the 'appearances of truth and the faithful were justified in believing in them'.

From 1858 to 1860 Bernadette lived quietly with her family until the Curé of Lourdes and the Mayor decided it would be best for her to reside with the Sisters of Charity at Nevers, to avoid the undesirable public curiosity which the vision had evoked. In 1864 she was accepted as a prospective postulant of the Convent but her poor state of health delayed her reception for two years.

For thirteen years she lived and worked in the Convent as the humble Sr Marie Bernard, her health still no better. During the winter of 1877 her asthma returned, she coughed blood and there was a painful abscess on her right knee which caused it to swell alarmingly. She made her perpetual vows on 22 September 1878 and on 28 March the following year she received the Last Sacraments. In the following Holy Week the temptations of the devil were added to her bodily sufferings, but she invoked the name of Jesus 'and it all went away'. On 16 April 1879 she calmly expired while clutching her beloved crucifix and saying the Hail Mary.

In the mother house at Nevers there is a coffin of gold and glass; in it lies the incorrupt body of Bernadette clad in the black habit of her order. A childlike figure but not the figure of a child. It is the figure of a Saint.

Lourdes today is a place of miracles. Yet its greatest miracle is the faith, hope and love of the pilgrims who come to pray at the shrine for the salvation of souls in this tormented world.

St John Nepomucen
(AD 1383)
May 16

He should truly be styled 'The defender of the seal of the confessional' because it was his courage in defending this holy Sacrament that eventually cost him his life. Born in 1330 at Nepomuc, near Prague, he was regarded as the fruit of his virtuous parents' prayers. Soon after his birth his life was despaired of, but he recovered in answer to entreaties made to the Blessed Virgin Mary and in gratitude he was consecrated to the service of God. His parents gave him the very best education to which he responded with goodness and an extraordinary application to his studies.

At the University of Prague (founded in 1356 by Emperor Charles IV of Germany and King of Bohemia) he excelled in philosophy, divinity and canon law, to which he added solitude, fasting, prayer and penance so that he might fulfil his desire to become a priest. Eventually he was ordained and the parish of Our Lady of Tein was committed to his care, with amazing results – people from near and far flocked to hear him preach, including students by the thousand, and the whole city was transformed.

The Emperor Charles, having reigned for thirty-two years and renowned for his wisdom and piety died in Prague in 1378. He was succeeded by Wenceslas, his sixteen-year-old son in the following year but unlike his father he proved to be both savage and vicious. Intrigued by the holy reputation of John, the new Emperor invited him to preach at court. So impressed was he that he offered him the bishopric of Leitomeritz but John, in humility, refused; in fact he refused all attempts to promote him. Yet the more he refused the esteem of men, the more it followed him, and eventually, he accepted the office of almoner of the court because it gave him greater latitude as a preacher and in caring for the poor.

The Empress Jane, holy and virtuous, chose him as her spiritual director – she needed a living saint to help her cope with the brutal Emperor and with his support she was able to suffer her afflictions with patience and joy. Following John's advice she became extremely religious, spending whole days in prayer and meditation, serving the poor, hearing Mass and receiving the Sacraments.

The Emperor was not pleased by her extravagant piety and he became suspicious and jealous despite her tenderness towards him. So distrustful was he that he endeavoured to extort from the priest what she had disclosed to him in the confessional. John was horrified and explained to the Emperor that to do so would be a sacrilege. The Emperor raged but to no avail, so he retreated into a dark and ominous silence.

One day at dinner, the tyrant Emperor finding a fowl not roasted to his liking ordered that the cook should be roasted alive. When John found out about this the unfortunate cook was already roasting on the fire. He begged the Emperor for mercy for him but in vain. John persisted in his pleas and the Emperor ordered him to be thrown into a dungeon, but John was convinced that the true reason for his suffering was because he would not disclose to the Emperor the confession of the Empress.

Some days later John was unexpectedly released, with an apology from the Emperor for the sufferings he had endured and an invitation to dine at court the next day. Here he was treated with esteem and kindness, then after the banquet the Emperor engaged him in conversation on mundane matters for a while, culminating in a promise of honours and riches if he would lay open the confession of the Empress. Refusal would mean horrific torture, then death.

John again tried to convince the Emperor of the sanctity of the secrecy of the confessional. The Emperor refused to listen and ordered him to be taken back to prison. Here John was tortured unmercifully, stretched on a rack and burning torches applied to the most tender parts of his body. He bore it all with the names of Jesus and Mary on his lips and Our Lord visited his servant to comfort and sustain him. When he was finally released from the rack he was left half dead.

In answer to entreaties from the Empress, John was released from prison and again appeared at court, yet despite the good humour of the Emperor he prepared himself for death. Returning from a pilgrimage at the shrine of the Blessed virgin Mary at Buntzel he was arrested. Taken before the Emperor he was again given the choice of breaking the silence of the confessional, or death. John made no reply. The obsessed Emperor cried out in fury: 'Take him away and throw him into the river! But after it is dark so that his execution shall not be known to the people.'

The barbarous order was executed. John's hands and feet were bound, and on 16 May 1383 he was thrown off a bridge into the River Muldaw. As soon as he hit the water a heavenly light appeared over him as he floated down the river, the light drawing crowds of people to the riverbank.

The Empress, seeing the heavenly light on the river asked the Emperor what was happening. The Emperor, horrified when he realised his murderous intrigue had been exposed fled distracted to his country house, forbidding anyone to follow him. In the morning, the executioners betrayed the guilty secret and the whole city flocked to venerate the body of the martyr, to kiss the hands and the feet, to beg for relics, his prayers and intercession. Despite the obstructive efforts of the Emperor, his body was taken to the cathedral then reverently interred with this epitaph: *Under this stone lies the body of the most venerable and most glorious Thaumaturgus JOHN NEPOMUCEN, Doctor, Canon of this church, and confessor of the Empress, who, because he had faithfully kept the seal of confession, was cruelly tormented and thrown from the Bridge of Prague into the River Muldaw, by the orders of Wenceslas IV, Emperor and King of Bohemia, son of Charles IV, 1383.*

The Empress died a happy and a holy death in the year 1387. The Emperor eventually returned to the city after months in exile at the Castle of Zebac, to continue his former dissolute life until eventually, his kingdom torn apart by civil wars and maladministration, he died of apoplexy unrepentant. For the next hundred years the kingdom suffered from cruel wars, bloodshed, plunder, sacrilege and every other calamity.

Many miracles were wrought at the intercession of the martyr, and at his tomb, ever protected by providence. In 1618 attempts were made by the Calvinists to destroy the tomb of the martyr, but those who sought to desecrate were deterred when some were struck dead on the spot.

On 14 April 1719 the martyr's tomb was opened after three hundred and thirty years. The flesh was consumed yet the bones were still perfectly joined together, with the marks of his fall into the river still visible. His tongue was found to be fresh and free from corruption as if it were still alive.

'A special providence watches over the fidelity of the sacred seal of the confessional. Without this indispensable secrecy the very precept and obligation ceases. It is unheard of that sins disclosed by confession should be divulged, lest others should be deterred from confessing.'

St Maurice and his Companions

(AD 286)
September 22

The emperor Diocletian was no enemy of the Christians in the early years of his reign and many were employed by him in the upper tiers of government, yet in certain quarters they were still persecuted. Maximian, a commander in the Roman Legions was one of the worst of these persecutors and responsible for the blood of many martyrs.

The Thebean Legion was sent by Diocletian to join his armies for the expedition into France. Maximian, after crossing the Alps halted his armies for rest after the rigorous march, with some detachments sent to Triers. The Thebean Legion was encamped at Agaunum, now called St Maurice and at this time Maximian ordered his armies to join in offering sacrifice to the gods for their success in the expedition.

The Thebean Legion refused to sacrifice despite repeated orders sent from the emperor, who eventually commanded them to be decimated. So every tenth soldier was put to death with the rest shouting encouragement and exhorting them to persevere in the Faith. A second decimation was ordered unless the soldiers obeyed orders to sacrifice but they boldly proclaimed that they would suffer any torments rather than abandon their holy religion. The slaughter began again, this time the victims being encouraged by three of their senior officers: Maurice, Exuperius and Candidus.

The emperor was furious and threatened that if they continued to disobey not one of them would escape death. The soldiers of the Legion, advised by Maurice and the other senior officers answered: 'We are your soldiers but we are also servants of the one true God. We owe you military service and obedience but we cannot renounce him who is our Creator and Master – and also yours, even if you reject him. You command us to offer sacrifice to false gods but how can we? We are Christians. We worship God the Father the author of all things and his Son our Lord Jesus Christ. We have seen our companions slain but we do not lament them – they have gone to their eternal reward. We will not resist even though we are fully armed because we would rather die innocent than live by sin.'

The Legion consisted of over 6,000 men who could have sold their lives dearly if they had so desired, but now they showed more courage than in any battles of the past. Maximian, having given up trying to make them change their minds ordered his whole army to surround them and cut them to pieces. They offered no resistance, allowing themselves to be butchered like sheep, only opening their mouths to encourage each other; not one of them failed in this moment of ultimate courage.

The ground was awash with blood, with bodies and limbs and when the slaughter was over Maximian gave the victim's possessions to their executioners. The soldiers were celebrating when Victor, a veteran soldier happened to pass by. They invited him to join them in their celebrations but he refused; the soldiers were suspicious and they asked him if he was, perhaps, a Christian. He answered that he was and always would be. The soldiers instantly killed him.

Ursus and Victor, two Christians who had crawled away from the massacre were discovered at Solodora, now Soleure, and butchered on the spot.

A fighting soldier who simply allows himself to be slaughtered displays a unique badge of courage rarely seen. A courage which goes against all his training and the basic instinct for survival. Truly a courage inspired by Christ himself, the Lamb nailed to the cross on Calvary.

These martyrs are styled 'The Happy Legion'.

St Germaine Cousin
(1579-1601)
June 15

Born at the little village of Pibrac just ten miles from Toulouse, Germaine Cousin did not exactly have the best start in life; one of her hands was deformed and she suffered from scrofula. There was no sovereign touch to cure her affliction even though monarchs from St Louis down to Charles X had, on occasion, performed the ceremony.

Calamity came early into her life: Germaine's mother died but her father soon married again, to a woman who proved to be the hardest of hard-hearted stepmothers. The new Madame Cousin, as married women of noble rank were styled in France, decided to segregate little Germaine from the rest of the children in case of infection. Her home was now a stable, then later a garret, her bed was of straw and leaves; during the day she looked after the sheep.

With time on her hands Germaine spent it wisely, in prayer. Unable to read, her Rosary Beads were her book to increase her devotion to our Blessed Lady. She heard Mass daily, received Holy Communion on feast days and gave religious instruction to the peasant children of the district. Always charitable to the poor, she saved from her own meagre fare what she could to give to them. It is related that some food she had put aside for the poor was hidden by her harsh stepmother, yet it blossomed into beautiful flowers.

It is also recorded that on more than one occasion she walked across the waters of the flooded river on her way to Mass. Yet to some, the devotions of this young hermit were regarded as a joke, until they at last realised there were genuine signs of holiness and in the poor little shepherdess they possessed a living saint. The villagers were not the only ones to learn a lesson; her father realised the wrongs he had permitted to be done to his daughter and ordered his wife to treat Germaine as one of the family.

But it is said that prisoners, after long years of confinement often become attached to their cells and so it was with Germaine. She had come to look upon her life of solitary pastoral care and her communing with God as the greatest blessing of her life. Her existence was wrapped in divine contemplation and the comforts of home were a poor compensation for celestial delights. It was fitting that the girl who had lived a life of hardship and neglect, even in the midst of her own family, should leave this world unnoticed.

Germaine Cousin, who had experienced twenty-two years of grief and sorrows which would have broken the hearts of the strongest, was found dead on her bed of leaves by her father in the summer of 1601. The people of Pibrac wanted her body to be close to them so her remains were interred in the parish church near the pulpit. Forty-three years later, her coffin had risen almost to the level of the floor of the church and her body inside was found to be incorrupt! Her wooden coffin was enclosed in one of lead, in thanksgiving from a Madame de Beauregard who had been cured of a dangerous ulcer by the intercession of this holy girl.

During the Revolution in 1793, the body was dragged from its coffin by a gang of Jacobins and thrown into a pit of quicklime and water. It was later recovered unharmed and restored to its original resting place, to be a source of various miracles and spiritual favours throughout the years, in testimony of the holiness of the little shepherdess.

Blessed Andrew Bobola
(1590?-1657)
May 23

It would seem that Poland has forever been a country troubled by all kinds of political divisions. In the sixteenth century there were 82,000 petty tyrants lording it over the land with the peasants kept in bondage. Yet Poland has always been, basically, devoutly Catholic though at this time some of the nobility adopted the tenets of Luther, Zwingly and Calvin, no doubt with a view to plundering the treasures of the Catholic Church. Archbishop Uchanski, the Primate of Poland deserted to Protestantism and split the Church right down the middle.

Cardinal Stanislaus Hosius did much to stem the flow into error but the major force in preserving the Faith were the Jesuits, the legacy of the work of St Peter Canisius. On 31 July 1611 Andrew Bobola was admitted as a novice to the Society of Jesus at Vilna. His parents were of the ruling class, fervent Catholics and decided their son would enter religion. Andrew, after long years of study was ordained priest on 22 March 1622. Well versed in scholastic philosophy and theology he was a powerful advocate against the prevailing errors of the day.

The plague hit the city of Vilna in the year 1625 and Fr Bobola and his brethren worked untiringly, day and night among the sick. Eight brethren of the Society died, but Fr Bobola was spared to glorify God at a later date. He was transferred to Bobruisk and appointed Superior of the Jesuit house there, but towards the end of his stay wild nomadic tribes of the Ukraine rose up against their overlords and the Cossacks took a horrible revenge on those who had oppressed them.

The Cossacks now turned their attentions to Poland, to overthrow the Catholic Church and set up the Greek Schismatic Church in its place; a bloodbath was imminent. The Patriarch of Constantinople sent Hetman Bogdan, the Cossack leader, a consecrated sabre and his blessings. On the Catholic side, Pope Innocent X dispatched a consecrated sword and helmet to John Casimir, the King of Poland. On 30 June 1653 the great Battle of Berestesko was fought and the Cossacks were routed, but that was not to be the end of the matter. The Russians under Czar Alexis Michaleovitch allied themselves with the Cossacks to crush Poland, which was also threatened by a Swedish army under the command of Charles Gusavus.

This schismatic crusade was met by a Catholic call to arms and from every village and town the youth of the country emerged to defend the religion of the Fatherland. Fr Bobola was sent to Pinsk in the Province of Lithuania where the greatest trouble was expected. The town was owned by Prince Radziwill, a nobleman, patriot and zealous Catholic. He had founded a Jesuit College in the town to strengthen the Faith. Fr Bobola was placed in charge and immediately set to work with a missionary zeal, to set up Catechism classes, to spend long hours in the confessional and to evangelise the surrounding districts; many were won back to the Faith. His successes greatly exasperated the local Greek clergy, so to rid themselves of these 'Latin priests' they called in the Cossacks, then in the region of Pinsk.

In 1657, these barbaric horsemen began their gruesome work by beheading Fr Muffon. Other Fathers barely had time to escape, but the search was on to find Fr Bobola who had departed to Janow, not to escape but to continue his ministry. He knew he was in danger yet he did not try to conceal himself, and while driving a carriage near the village of Poredelno he was overtaken by Cossacks and taken prisoner.

His savage captors overwhelmed him with cruelty, sabres slashed and lances pierced. He was scourged, then dragged across the rough ground all the way to Janow where his mangled, half-dead body was displayed to the terrified people. At the instigation of Assavoula, the Cossack chief he was subjected to fresh torments. His hands were slashed in mockery of his priestly anointing, his hair and skin were cut from his head to make a gruesome monk's tonsure while the rest of his body was flayed.

And all this time Fr Bobola continued to pray for his barbarous executioners while he committed his own soul to God. Assavoula finally tired of the horror and bloodshed put an end to the priest's sufferings with a single thrust from his own sword.

When the Cossacks had departed, the villagers recovered the mutilated remains of the martyr and after public veneration at Janow, they were taken back to Pinsk, to be interred in the Chapel of the Jesuit College.

In 1702, almost fifty years after his death, the remains of Fr Bobola were found to be still incorrupt.

Blessed Margaret Clitherow
(1553-1586)
March 25

The name of Margaret Clitherow shines out like a glorious star among the Catholics of England who suffered for the Faith as Queen Elizabeth I continued the persecutions begun by her father, Henry VIII and the Reformation.

Born in 1553, Margaret was the daughter of Thomas Middleton, the Sheriff of York, who unfortunately died when she was still very young. In July 1571 she married John Clitherow, a lapsed Catholic but a rich butcher and City Chamberlain. They lived in a house at 36, The Shambles, a street in the city of York.

The year 1574 was significant for Margaret; she had two children – Henry aged two and baby Anne – and she became a Catholic, to lead a life of holiness and mortification with exemplary devotion to the ancient Faith. The same year, missionary priests were beginning to arrive in England from the English College at Douai which had been set up in 1568. Margaret met one of the priests and she was to spend the rest of her life helping them. Her house became one of the chief Mass centres in York, she ran a school for Catholic children yet she remained the devoted wife (of a quite supportive husband) and mother with all the old-fashioned time-consuming duties of keeping house.

In 1584 she secretly arranged for her son Henry, now aged twelve to go to the English College at Douai.

Then in 1585 the horrendous Statute 27 was passed by Elizabeth making it a crime punishable by death to contact or harbour a Catholic priest. Margaret's friends begged her to give up her work for the Faith but she replied: 'If God's priests ask for my help, I will never refuse them.'

Margaret's persistent absence from the Parish Church had not gone unnoticed by the authorities (in 1576 she had been sentenced to two years in prison for refusing to attend) and in 1586 they decided to act. The Sheriff of York and his priest hunters raided Margaret's house but they were unable to uncover any incriminating evidence. Then disaster struck for Margaret. The Sheriff succeeded in terrorising a fourteen-year-old Flemish servant boy so much that he cracked, to reveal a secret hiding place with vestments, chalice and other 'massing stuffe'. Margaret was arrested.

She was committed for trial at the York Lent Assizes and charged with 'harbouring priests, traitors to the Queen's Majesty'. Margaret replied, 'I have never harboured anyone but the Queen's friends.' Yet she knew the court was set on her death and, not wishing her children and servants (the Crown's only witnesses against her) to testify and wanting to save a jury from the guilt of sharing in her death, she refused trial by jury. The alternative was to be pressed to death. When the horrific sentence was announced her courage was confirmed in her words: 'Whatever God sends, it shall be welcome to me.' And so she gave up husband and children, home and friends, even life itself for her love of the Faith and Our Lord Jesus Christ.

On Friday 25 March 1586 at eight o'clock in the morning the gory ritual began. Margaret walked barefoot to the Tolbooth Prison in York carrying a white garment over her arm; with her were four Sheriffs, four executioners and four lady friends. Inside the dungeon she pleaded that she should not be stripped but the Sheriff refused her request. The women gathered round, then as she lay on the ground the white garment was placed over her.

She was stretched out in the form of a cross, limbs tied to stakes in the floor and a sharp stone placed under her back. A door was laid on top of her and the executioners began heaving weights on to it, then more weights to almost a thousand pounds. Despite the excruciating pain Margaret thanked God for her death and prayed for the Queen that she might turn to the true Faith. As her end drew near she cried out, 'Jesus, Jesus, Jesus, have mercy on me!' The moaning ceased, all was quiet and this brave martyr had gone to her reward.

Margaret was thirty-three years of age and almost certainly pregnant, so this was the unique martyrdom of a mother and her unborn child. Her body was eventually rescued by the faithful; but its place of burial is unknown, but a hand, shrivelled but intact is a sacred relic in the Bar Convent, York.

The faith of Margaret Clitherow was to live on in her children. William and Henry became priests in Douai and her daughter Anne joined the convent of St Ursula at Louvain. Her husband John was banished from England.

St Lawrence

(AD 258)

August 10

The date of his birth is not known, yet it would seem that the place of his birth was somewhere in Spain. Due to his extraordinary virtue as a youth he was recommended to Sixtus, the Archdeacon of Rome who took him under his protection, instructed him in the study of holy Scripture and in the art of Christian perfection.

In the year 257 Sixtus was elected Pope (the second to bear the name) and even though Lawrence was still very young he ordained him deacon and appointed him to be one of the seven deacons who served in the Roman Church. Among his duties was care of the treasury and the distribution of alms to the poor.

In the same year, the Emperor Valerian began a bloody persecution against the Church and Sixtus II was one of his first victims. As he was led to his execution the devoted Lawrence followed, distraught that he was not to die with his master. The holy Pope was moved to compassion and tenderness at the sight of his grief and comforting him he said, 'I do not leave you, my son; but a greater trial and a more glorious victory awaits you who are brave and in the vigour of youth. You shall be with me in three days.' He then instructed him to immediately distribute all the treasures of the Church among the poor so they would not fall into the hands of the persecutors.

Lawrence was overjoyed that he was to follow his master into martyrdom. He gathered together as many poor people as he could find and gave them all the money he had. He raised even more money from the sale of the gold and silver vessels of the Church and just in time, for the prefect of Rome summoned Lawrence to inform him that he was to hand over to the authorities all the wealth of the Church.

Lawrence replied that the riches of the Church were truly astounding, but he would require three days to gather them all together. No doubt the prefect was impressed… and Lawrence could afford a wry smile.

In those three days Lawrence gathered together thousands of lepers, the blind and the sick and the poor, orphans and widows and the aged, to take them to the prefect and say, 'These are the true treasures of the Church. A Church that is truly rich in the treasures of God and far richer than your Emperor.'

The prefect was far from pleased, in fact he was furious! 'You mock me!' he cried in a rage. 'And you insult the Roman power. I know of your desire to die and follow your master – that is your vanity! You will die but you will not die immediately; I will protract your tortures, your death will be slow and bitter.' With that he ordered a gridiron to be made while Lawrence was held in captivity.

Romanus, a soldier in Rome at the time of Lawrence's tribulations was overwhelmed by his youthful bravery; so inspired that he decided to become a Christian. By what must have been an act of amazing faith he was instructed by Lawrence and baptised. Then in an act of reckless spiritual joy he loudly proclaimed his new-found faith, only to be arrested, condemned and beheaded the day before his guide and master.

The prefect carried out his threat. Lawrence was stripped, lashed to the gridiron and hung over a slow fire. The watching Christians saw his face bathed in a celestial light and his roasting flesh exuded a sweet odour, yet unbelievers saw and sensed nothing.

So great was his love for God that the torments of Lawrence, his pain and agony were transformed into spiritual serenity and such was his tranquillity that he smiled and said, 'Let my body be turned, one side is roasted enough!'

As he was slowly roasted to death, Lawrence prayed in the names of St Peter and St Paul for the conversion of the city of Rome. His prayer would be eventually answered yet the conversion began almost immediately. A number of Senators who were present when he finally gave up his soul to God became Christians on the spot. These noblemen took the martyr's body to give it a honourable burial in the Veran field near the road to Tibur on 10 August 258.

Through the intercession of St Lawrence many miracles were wrought in this great city which was to become the centre of Christianity. He was the young martyr who laughed in the face of death, a death that was to become the death of idolatry in Rome.

St Mary Magdalen
(AD 84)
July 22

This illustrious lady could truly be styled 'The great penitent'. Her rise from a pit of iniquity to the heights of sanctity has rarely been seen and seldom equalled. Her debaucheries had rendered her name infamous in the city of Nain in Galilee (prostitutes were a rarity in the sparsely populated and strict community), but like the Prodigal Son, she was eventually to realise the error of her ways.

Not long after Jesus had raised to life the son of a widow in Nain, he was invited to dinner by Simon the Pharisee. Mary was determined to meet Jesus to beg his forgiveness and, courageously, in public. Entering the room she knelt before Jesus; to wash his feet with her tears, drying them with her hair then tenderly kissing them. Mary then anointed his feet with a rich perfumed essence she had brought with her in an alabaster jar.

Jesus, who had himself inspired her to contrition, looked mercifully on her. The Pharisee was shocked to see this infamous sinner in his house and kneeling at the feet of Jesus, his honoured guest. He concluded in his mind that Jesus couldn't be much of a prophet if he didn't know all about this scandalous woman.

But Jesus knew exactly what he was thinking and seeing the pride in his heart he decided to cure his rash judgement with a parable to convince him that she, to whom so much had been forgiven, loved God all the more and was more acceptable to him.

'Simon,' said Jesus, 'I have something to say to you. A certain creditor had two debtors; one owed him five hundred denarii, and another fifty. When they could not pay, he forgave them both. Now which of them will love him more?'

'The one, I suppose,' Simon answered, 'to whom he forgave more.'

'Do you see this woman?' Jesus said, turning towards her. 'I entered your house, you gave me no water for my feet, but she has wet my feet with her tears and wiped them with her hair. You gave me no kiss, but from the time I came in she has not ceased to kiss my feet. You did not anoint my head with oil, but she has anointed my feet with ointment. Therefore I tell you, her sins, which are many, are forgiven, for she loved much; but he who is forgiven little loves little.' Then he said to Mary, 'Your sins are forgiven.'

Those who were at table with him began to say among themselves, 'Who is this who even forgives sins?' But Jesus said to Mary, 'Your faith has saved you, go in peace.'

From that moment Mary followed Jesus faithfully, even to his crucifixion where she stood at the foot of the cross with Mary his holy mother. How she must have suffered at the cruel death of the one who had forgiven her and loved her so much. And when the end came she helped to bury him.

The dawn of the first Easter Sunday found Mary Magdalen, Joanna, Mary the mother of James, and other devout women arriving at the entrance of the sepulchre. They carried spices, for it was their intention to embalm the body of Jesus, yet they were concerned about how they would roll away the great stone which had sealed the tomb. A surprise awaited them – the stone was already rolled away but when they looked in there was no body and, another surprise, there were two angels dressed in shining white garments. One of them told the women not to fear, Jesus had risen and they were to tell the Apostles.

Mary Magdalen ran to inform Peter and John the Beloved Disciple. The Apostles, having seen the empty tomb believed all that Mary had told them and in great astonishment returned to Jerusalem to inform the other disciples. Mary didn't go with them but she kept a lone and tearful vigil outside the sepulchre. Then, in her loving desire to see Jesus again, either dead or alive, she stooped low to look again into the tomb. There she saw two angels and one of them said to her, 'Woman, why do you weep?'

She replied, 'Because they have taken away my Lord and I do not know where they have laid him.' Not even the surprise of this apparition nor the brightness and the glory of these heavenly messengers could divert her attention from the Jesus she loved so much.

Mary then turned away from the entrance to see Jesus himself standing close to her, but she thought he was the gardener. He asked her why she wept, and what she sought.

She said to him, 'If you have taken him away, tell me where you have laid him and I will take him away.'

Jesus said, 'Mary.' And instantly she recognised him.

Mary exclaimed, 'Rabboni!', teacher. Then overwhelmed with joy she threw herself at his feet and would have embraced him but he said, 'Do not hold me; for I am not yet ascended to my Father. But go to my brethren and say to them: I ascend to my Father and to your Father, to my God and to your God.'

It is an ancient and popular tradition among the inhabitants of Provence in France that Mary Magdalen, Martha and Lazarus, with other disciples, were expelled by the Jews after the ascension of Our Lord. They put to sea and landed at Marseilles; they founded the Church there and Lazarus became the first bishop of the city.

In the thirteenth century the relics of these saints were discovered, those of Mary Magdalen at a place now called St Maximin's, those of St Martha at Tarascon on the Rhone, the others in Marseilles. The relics were proved genuine by the artefacts found with them.

In 1660 the relics of the saints were transferred to the subterranean chapel at St Maximin's; the head of St Mary Magdalen was set in a gold case and encrusted with large diamonds, surmounted by the royal crown of Charles II, King of Sicily and Naples,

The life of St Mary Magdalen is a constant source of encouragement to all sinners, a loving example of God's great mercy to all who genuinely and humbly repent, however great the sin. Her great love for Jesus was rewarded when it was not to Peter nor John the beloved disciple nor to any of the Apostles or disciples, nor to any of the other holy men and women that Jesus first appeared after his resurrection, but to Mary, the repentant sinner.

Blessed Padre Pio
(1887-1968)

Francesco Forgione, or Padre Pio as he was later to become was born on 25 May 1887 in the small, grey stone village of Pietrelcina near Benevento in southern Italy.

His parents, Orazio Forgione and Maria Giuseppa De Nunzio were poor peasants; there were eight children and three of them died in infancy.

As early as the age of five, Francesco began to experience ecstasies and assaults from the devil. In the village church of St Anne's he had a vision of the Sacred Heart. Later, he was to say that he had felt hands on his head as if accepting the decision he had already made to devote his life to God.

One day, this quiet, deeply religious little boy was with his father watching his brother Michele working in the fields under the hot Italian sun. His father said to him, 'I am never going to let you see the sun.'

Francesco asked his father what he meant.

His father told him that he wanted him to study to become a monk and he intended to go to New York to earn the money to make this possible.

His first tutor was not a success, but under his next tutor, Maestro Caccavo, Francesco made rapid progress in his studies.

In 1902 Francesco was accepted in the Capuchin monastery at Marcone, but the rigorous life took its toll on his always delicate health and he was sent to

St Elia, in Panisi, took the name of Pio and remained for the next four years.

In spite of the change of air his health did not improve. He suffered frequent bouts of fever and nausea yet he was always cheerful. His hours in penance and prayer were tormented by vicious attacks from evil spirits, as if the powers of darkness were trying to destroy this frail young man who was going to be a powerful adversary. Pio told only his confessor of these visitations.

Pio's cell was often trashed in his absence. There were times when he found himself surrounded by hideous monsters who jeered at him and challenged him to fight. The demons came in various guises: one appeared as his old confessor who exhorted him to give up his life of prayer and penance, assuring him that God did not approve of his way of life.

Pio was shocked and bewildered. '*Viva Gesù!*' he cried. The apparition disappeared immediately, leaving behind a sulphurous smell.

Pio's health deteriorated even further and a doctor declared him to be tubercular. Despite this, he was ordained priest on 10 August 1910 in the cathedral of Benevento, while his father was in America,

Padre Pio was sent to Foggia but his health was no better, so he went home to rest. It was during this time that he had an indication of what would happen later in his life – a stinging like that of bees in his hands. It was September 1915 and his village was commemorating the Stigmata of St Francis of Assisi.

Italy became involved in World War I and Padre Pio was called up for military service in the Medical Corps.

He was soon discharged due to his medical condition and sent by his religious superiors to San Giovanni Rotondo, where he was to spend the rest of his life. This isolated monastery is situated in a barren district on the Gargant Peninsula overlooking the Adriatic Sea. Its highest point is Monte Calvo, with a cave on its eastern side where, it is reputed, Archangel Michael routed the devil.

Padre Pio settled down to a life of prayer, penance and obscurity. He was devoted to the Blessed Virgin Mary and he lived with a rosary in his hands. In ecstasies he spoke to her, to his Guardian Angel, to the Holy Souls and to Jesus.

In September 1918 the Capuchin Fathers celebrated the Stigmata of St Francis of Assisi. The feast day fell on a Wednesday; the following Friday, Padre Pio was in the choir stalls making his thanksgiving after Mass when a piercing cry rent the air.

One of the monks ran to the choir to find Padre Pio bleeding profusely from five wounds: in his hands, his feet and side. His fellow monks carefully lifted him to take him back to his cell where he begged them to keep it a secret.

Somehow the 'secret' quickly spread. People flooded in, drawn across this wild region to see 'The Saint' and kneel before him in the confessional.

The Father Provincial of the Capuchins of Foggia had the wounds photographed and copies sent to the Vatican, but for the next ten years Padre Pio was to remain in official obscurity.

Doctor Luigi Romanelli examined the wounds, there were more investigations and attempted cures, but nothing would stop the bleeding yet neither did they become infected. Eventually Padre Pio was left in peace, his painful wounds bandaged and covered with mittens, yet the tuberculosis which had troubled him for many years had miraculously disappeared.

His day began at 3.30 in the morning with Mass at 5.30, yet the crowds had gathered at 2.00 a.m. to wait for his Mass and their own confessions. For some there was a wait of ten days despite the fact that Padre Pio spent between twelve and eighteen hours a day in the confessional.

Eating only one meal a day was not enough to make up for the amount of blood he lost from his wounds. Ill with stomach trouble, he took only a little water in eight days, but when he had recovered he found he had put on weight. In 1923 he had a hernia operation but refused anaesthetic. He had also lost the frail appearance of his youth: hair and beard mottled in grey, eyes bright with the fire of the Apostles.

Devotion spread; hundreds of letters arrived every day full of requests for prayers and counsel and favours, yet because of his wounds he could not reply personally. Padre Pio continued his vocation to save souls with his prayers and sufferings and guidance in the confessional. He was blessed with supernatural gifts: bilocation, knowledge of languages, invisibility, celestial perfume, prophecy, the ability to read hearts and souls, command of the elements and the working of miracles.

Throughout the years of his life, innumerable miracles of body and soul have been attributed to the intercession of Padre Pio.

He prayed and a little girl born without pupils in her eyes could see; the holy man touched a hopeless cripple and he walked away. A friend, after visiting Padre Pio had to walk home in the pouring rain – and didn't get wet. In confession, a woman for her penance was told to go home and look down the well in her garden, where she saw the face of the child she had aborted. An Italian lady was waiting to have a leg amputated; Padre Pio appeared to her and the leg was completely healed. A woman developed pneumonia and the intercession of Padre Pio was requested. He predicted her cure would take place at the ringing of the Easter bells. It did! A man suffering from ulcers in his stomach was cured by the touch of Padre Pio's hand. A mysterious monk appeared to drag an Italian soldier away from a violent explosion… it was Padre Pio. The list would seem to be endless.

In 1936 he foretold the death of the King of England even though the newspapers had reported that he was only suffering from a mild form of influenza. During World War II he defended the village of San Giovanni from attack by American bombers when his image miraculously appeared in the sky in front of the planes.

There are numerous examples given of his bi-location. He was reliably sighted in the crypt of St Peter's, at the tomb of Pius X, in Loretto, even in Milwaukee U.S.A., and he had never left his monastery.

The duration of the stigmata of Padre Pio was the longest ever recorded among the sixty or so acknowledged stigmatists – from 1918 to 1968. He died, renowned for the stigmata which modern science could never explain. Neither could it explain the other incredible gifts with which he was blessed, because these were things of God.

The night before he died, Padre Pio said his last Mass, hardly able to breathe. In the evening he was helped to his window to greet the visitors below by waving a white handkerchief. The crowd responded, the shutters were closed. In the night, sick and trembling, he made his last confession and renewed his Religious Vows. He died at 2.30 a.m. on 23 September 1968 with the words *Gesù* and *Maria* on his lips.

In the months preceding his death, the stigmata had begun to fade and with his death, no trace of the wounds remained.

His funeral, on a beautiful sunny day in San Giovanni Rotondo was attended by something like 100,000 people from all over the world. He was laid to rest in a dark, oblong tomb in the new church of San Giovanni.

Padre Pio was the first priest to receive the stigmata and was regarded by many as a legend in his own lifetime. He was a worthy successor of St Francis of Assisi, a fellow Capuchin monk and the first to receive the stigmata – this amazing token of Christ's love and affection.

He was beatified on 2 May 1999 by Pope John Paul II, witnessed by a crowd of 300,000 people packed into St Peter's Square. The Pope, who had been a pilgrim to Padre Pio's monastery in San Giovanni Rotondo said, 'I thank God for allowing me today to enter the name of Padre Pio in the book of the blessed.'

To beg the prayers of the Saints

O merciful God, let the glorious intercession of thy saints assist us; above all, the most blessed Virgin Mary, Mother of thy only begotten Son, and thy holy Apostles Peter and Paul, to whose patronage we humbly recommend this our land. Be mindful of our fathers, Eleutherius, Celestine and Gregory, bishops of the holy city; of Augustine, Columba and Aidan, who delivered to us inviolate the faith of the holy Roman Church. Remember our holy martyrs, who shed their blood for Christ: especially our first martyr, St Alban, and thy most glorious bishop, St Thomas of Canterbury. Remember all those holy confessors, bishops and kings, all those holy monks and hermits, all those holy virgins and widows, who made this once an island of saints, illustrious by their glorious merits and virtues. Let not their memory perish from before thee, O Lord, but let their supplication enter daily into thy sight. And do thou, who didst so often spare thy sinful people for the sake of Abraham, Isaac, and Jacob, now, also moved by the prayers of our fathers reigning with thee, have mercy upon us, save thy people, and bless thy inheritance and suffer not those souls to perish, which your Son has redeemed with his most precious blood. Who lives and reigns with you, world without end.

Amen

Let us pray

O loving Lord Jesus, when you were hanging an the cross, you did commend us all, in the person of your disciple John to your most sweet Mother, that we might find in her our own refuge, our solace and our hope; look graciously upon our beloved land, and on those who are bereaved of so powerful a patronage; that, acknowledging once more the dignity of this holy Virgin, they may honour and venerate her with all affection and devotion, and own her as Queen and Mother. May her sweet name be lisped by little ones, and linger on the lips of the aged and the dying; and may it be invoked by the afflicted, and hymned by the joyful, that this star of the sea being their protection and guide, all may come to the harbour of eternal salvation. Who lives and reigns, world without end.

Amen

The quest for sanctity is difficult; at times it would seem to be almost impossible, yet it is attainable. A difficult task is made easier if we have the assistance of someone who has done it all before. This is why the example of the saints who *have* attained sanctity is a constant encouragement for those who aim to follow in their footsteps.

Bibliography

Burdyszek, John, *Father Maximilian Kolbe: Fire Enkindled*, Clonmore & Reynolds Ltd, Dublin, 1954.

Carty, Charles Mortimer, *Padre Pio: The Stigmatist,* Tan Books and Publishers, Inc. 1973.

MacNiven-Johnston, Glynn, *Maria Goretti: Teenage Martyr*, Catholic Truth Society, London, 1997.

Tigar, Clement, *Forty Martyrs of England and Wales,* The Burleigh Press, Bristol, 1961.

Butler, Rev Alban, *Butler's Lives of the Saints*, Virtue & Company Ltd, London & Dublin, 1954.

Craig, Mary, *Maximilian Kolbe*, Catholic Truth Society, 1997.

Couve de Murville, M.N.L. *Karl Leisner*, Catholic Truth Society, 1997.